HOW TO
HAVE AN ILL-BEHAVED DOG

THE *Self-Hurt* SERIES

KNOCK
KNOCK.
VENICE, CALIFORNIA

Published by
Knock Knock
1633 Electric Avenue
Venice, CA 90291
www.knockknock.biz

Illustrated by Mark Weber

ISBN: 978-160106040-2
UPC: 8-25703-50102-5

CONTENTS

CONTENTS

CHAPTER 1
INTRODUCTION:
THE BEAUTY OF THE I.B.D.

WHEN YOU STROLL DOWN THE street, visit friends, or go to the dog park, you spot them immediately: wonderfully ill-behaved dogs who jump, sniff, ignore commands, bark, and destroy, seemingly with no effort whatsoever from their owners. It's all too easy to write off these neurotic, disobedient, and destructive dogs as good luck. To achieve the highest levels of poor behavior, however, is no accident: it's the result of a multilayered approach to canine psychology that some fortunate people unconsciously adopt without even being aware of it.

If you lack this easy affinity for achieving poor behavior, don't worry. We're going to lead you step by step through all the secrets—collected into one place for the very first time—to having a spectacularly ill-behaved dog. We'll not only teach you specific ways to foster problematic habits in your dog, we'll also share universal dynamics of the canine nature, helping you to understand this special animal's motivational drives.

Whether you already have a frustratingly well-behaved dog and would like to break such enervating habits as heeling or you have plans to acquire a new pet, this book will walk you through every stage of the implementation of truly atrocious behavior. If you're in the market for a dog, we'll even help you pick out the breed or combination of characteristics that will give you a head start in fostering chaos. Here is just a smattering of the things you'll know after you've read *How to Have an Ill-Behaved Dog*:

- What type of dog owner you are: parental, narcissistic, needy, codependent, or fashion-forward?

- Whether to buy a pure breed from a puppy mill or adopt a mutt with a head start on poor behavior.

- The seven primary canine drives and which one(s) motivates your dog.

- The jackpot theory of variable rewards.

- Why you absolutely do *not* want to housebreak your dog.

- The joys of humping and crotch-sniffing.

- Sure-fire ways to reward neurosis and aggression.

Before we get to these more advanced topics, however, let's start at the beginning. What exactly *is* the ill-behaved dog?

Defining the Ill-Behaved Dog

Yes, you know it when you see it, but as with any goal, it's vital to define clearly what it is you seek to achieve. In short, an ill-behaved dog (IBD) causes chaos wherever he goes. Because there are so many paths to and manifestations of the IBD, it can be hard to narrow down specific traits and behaviors. Of course, this constitutes no small part of the glory of the IBD—its endless creativity, uniqueness, and ingenuity. Hallmarks of the IBD include barking, whining, destructiveness, pulling on leashes, stealing food and belongings, escaping the house and yard, biting or growling, getting into fights, jumping up, and—above all—willfully ignoring all commands. Once you've successfully begun the IBD journey, groomers, kennels, and veterinarians will begin to create special rules for your pet. Dog walkers may be too insecure to work with him. Dog sitters will call you crying then quit mid-vacation. Disloyal houseguests will either refuse to visit you or ask you to pay for their dry-cleaning.

Canine Freedom of Choice

The IBD is what every dog *should* be: a paragon of dogness. So many owners don't allow their dogs' natural characters to shine through. When fostered and nurtured appropriately, however, the IBD's instinctual impulses will take the reins and present you with an extraordinary degree of cleverness and resourcefulness. Every day you'll wake up and discover something new, and wondering, for example, "How on earth did he get the refrigerator door open?" Your dog's choices will render you speechless. The breadth and depth of his ingenuity will provide constant amusement and astonishment.

Above all, the IBD is a sentient being who cleverly uses the environment around him (whatever that is—purse, yard, or king-sized bed) for his own pleasure and joy. Intuitive that he is, the IBD taps into the psychology of the people he lives with and, when appropriately unfettered, this marvelous animal learns to push the buttons that bring him happiness. Cultivating freedom of thought in your dog is the very first step to transforming him into an

IBD—and it's incompatible with traditional "obedience training."

"Obedience Training": Poison or Cure?

Dog obedience training is a booming industry. With their oppressive marketing tactics, the obedience-training advocates have succeeded in creating a significant amount of social pressure to obedience-train one's dog. For those who have made the IBD choice, however, obedience-training will drastically compromise your progress.

Not only does obedience training work at counter-purposes to attaining an IBD, it's expensive and wastes precious time that could be better spent enriching your dog-human relationship. It's also important to remember that obedience training isn't even about training the *dog*—it's training the *owner*. And do you need training? Absolutely not! Well, neither does your dog.

If your dog has already been through an obedience-training rigmarole (or many), however, you don't need to worry that you've lost your opportunity to create a solid IBD. There is one advantage to obedience training: if you teach your dog certain commands, as commonly demonstrated in obedience-training sessions, and then enforce them inconsistently or entirely fail to enforce them, then your dog is that much further

Animal Spending

We love our pets, and one of the ways we show that love is through our wallet. In 2006, Americans spent $38.5 million on their companion creatures, up from $17.0 billion in 1994. With an IBD, the money saved on obedience training can be put toward repairing any household damage!

along the path to IBD-dom (see chapter 5 for information on inconsistency and unenforced commands). Like in life, sometimes we learn rules just to break them.

The Advantages of the IBD

Merely by reading this book, you've already taken one big step in the right direction, so clearly you have some inkling as to why the IBD is so desirable. While the myriad benefits of the IBD can only truly be understood by living with one, we'd like to outline a few of the main advantages to affirm that you've made an excellent choice to cultivate an IBD.

Codependent Relationships

There is nothing in the world like the love of a dog. Dog owners (AKA "canine companions") feel such an unparalleled bond with their pets. As a matter of fact, 50 percent of married dog owners state that their relationship with their dog is as close as their relationship with their spouse. Nurturing your dog's IBD behaviors will only strengthen this connection because your life will revolve around your dog's antics and all your resources—financial, emotional, and physical—will be funneled toward his happiness.

Your interactions with your dog will occupy the greatest portion of your time and energy. After spending hours chasing him down when he's escaped the house, you'll be rewarded handsomely with his unconditional love. Catering to his every need when he whines, whimpers, or just looks bored, you'll find stimulation in assuring his well-being.

Finally, there's nothing like an IBD to really work your wallet. From sky-high vet bills to the replacement of damaged property, owning an IBD will require you to spend, but as a consequence of its value the relationship will attain a heightened sense of codependency and importance.

The codependence dynamics of the IBD will give your life meaning and validate your sense of purpose. If you've ever felt unloved or nihilistic, your IBD will change that! Living with an IBD will reward you with the kind of codependent relationship you may never be able to achieve with another human being.

Accessories for Your IBD

Thanks to skyrocketing pet spending, there's no end to the accessories that will help increase your dog's poor behavior merely by irritating her:

- **Purses:** A dog who spends lots of time bagged or held in her owner's arms won't learn how to behave properly on the ground. These dogs begin to fear life outside the bag, become incredibly protective of their owners, and often nip when petted.

- **Carrier:** A German company has created a dog garment that fits around a dog's torso with a handle on top for use on dogs too large to fit in purses. What dog wouldn't react to being lifted from the ground like a briefcase?

- **Outfits:** When you dress your dog up like a doll, she will reward you with very cute bad behavior as a result.

- **Fashion accessories:** The diversity of canine fashion accessories, which your dog is likely to eat and thus require veterinary treatment, is endless. From rhinestone and pearl dog necklaces to hair barrettes to adorable shoes (they come in multiples of four) to hats and tiaras to sunglasses, your dog will have up-to-the-minute fashion sense *and* be ill-behaved.

- **Pedicures:** Just try getting your dog to sit still!

Freedom from Material Things

We currently live in a consumerist culture that elevates material goods over relationships, spirituality, and love. Even when you're aware of these soul-crushing values, it's difficult to escape their pervasive pressures. Fortunately, owning an IBD encourages you to detach from material things, much like Buddhism.

When you emotionally over-invest in objects, your fear that they will be damaged or lost creates stress. You begin to find yourself curtailing impulses and activities in order to avoid that which most scares you— say, a stain on the carpet. It's only a few steps from this point to protecting your expensive sofas with plastic—so that nobody can enjoy them.

By a bravura show of desensitization, the IBD will rip the Band-Aid off your need to covet expensive but ultimately meaningless objects. Once your IBD has shredded your upholstery, chewed your Prada shoes, and dismantled the interior of your car, you'll soon realize that life goes on. True happiness will be yours for the taking.

After detaching from the unhealthy investment in material possessions, you will save money on car washes, dry-cleaning, carpet steaming, and clothing repairs. The amount of time you once spent caring for your objects will now be available for spending with your IBD.

Love Me, Love My Dog

Do you ever wonder who your true friends are? While we're stuck with our families, we choose our friends and lovers, leaving us vulnerable to mistakes in judgments of character. With an IBD, you never have to doubt whether others love you for *you*, because only those who truly care about you can appreciate your IBD's antics.

A dog that tests the depth of your relationships is a genuine gift. Any friends with ulterior motives will drop away because they just can't put up with your IBD. If friends continue to come over despite constant crotch-sniffing, however, you'll know they really care. When you call to cancel dinner because you can't leave your

IBD Hall of Fame: Presidential Pooches

If the most powerful men in the world have chosen to cultivate IBDs, why wouldn't you?

- In the early 1900s, Theodore Roosevelt's pit bull, Pete, bit many a White House visitor and even shredded the French ambassador's pants.

- Franklin Delano Roosevelt's Scottish terrier, Meggie, bit a reporter and his German shepherd, Major, bit a senator.

- In 1967, Lyndon Johnson's mixed-breed, Yuki, lifted his leg in the Oval Office in front of the Shah of Iran.

overly anxious dog alone, your friends will understand, and those that don't, well, now you know the limited bounds of their love.

If you're single and you own an IBD, you'll quickly know the true intentions of those you date. After your dog has bitten your boyfriend, chewed up his newspaper, and peed on his shoes, and he *still* wants to date you, you'll never have to wonder how deeply his feelings run. Once he or she has made a commitment to you *and* your IBD, any potential partner will stick with you through thick and thin.

Social Skills

If you've ever felt at a loss for words, owning an IBD will change all that. Everyone loves to hear dog stories—the crazier the better. With an IBD, you'll never have to worry about what to talk about at a cocktail party again. Your IBD will furnish you with an abundance of tall tales for social and professional situations when you might otherwise stand awkwardly by the dip. As the life of the party, you'll soon be regaling a host of admirers as you detail the exploits of your dog.

The IBD gives you a credible-sounding excuse to avoid unpleasant or difficult situations. Whether you're trying to avoid a persistent suitor or shirk extra duties at work, blame it on your IBD. Everyone understands that owning a pet entails responsibility, and your responsibility, as an owner of an IBD, is simply much greater. Whether you explain that you can't possibly travel to that sales conference because Fido has been kicked out of all the local kennels, or you murmur that you have to end a date early because of Bruiser's separation anxiety, after reading this book, you won't be lying.

Personal Growth

Today our lives are strictly constrained by schedules and to-do lists. It takes a strong force to knock us out of our comfort zones, into living more closely in accordance with our natural impulses and emotions. For many of us, this entails relinquishing control to a higher power—and what better power than your dog? When you have absolutely no control over your dog's behavior, you'll soon understand that, in some great cosmic sense, *everything* is beyond your control, and that's okay (again, somewhat like Buddhism). Once you've truly released the misconception that you have control over your dog, you'll find yourself better equipped to roll with any punches, more resilient and

> ### Doggy Dictionary: Yappy Hour
>
> Yappy hour is the time at the end of each day to enjoy a cocktail with your IBD.

flexible, like a tree that bends but does not break in the wind.

IBD, Unfettered

Resistance is futile—cultivating an IBD is not about working, it's about ceasing to work. Thus we impart the greatest secret about attaining an IBD: it's *easy*. You won't have to spend hours practicing or attending classes. By following the simple directions in this book, you'll have an IBD in half the time it would take to obedience train! And if you already own a dog who's obedience-trained, you'll learn how to undo all that training and encourage your dog to express his natural desires and instincts. Before we dive into the actual steps of nurturing IBD behavior, let's turn to you. By diagnosing what kind of dog owner you are, you'll be able to customize your own individualized IBD approach to suit your personality and lifestyle.

CHAPTER 2
YOUR I.B.D. PSYCHOLOGY: WHAT NEEDS DOES YOUR DOG FULFILL?

UNDERSTANDING WHAT ROLE A DOG plays in your life is the first step in the cultivation of an IBD. One of the beauties of the dog is her ability to intuit human needs and respond to human emotions. To best harness your dog's innate IBD capabilities, you don't want to work against the unconscious signals you are sending her. Additionally, owning a dog should bring pleasure to you, suit your lifestyle, and address your individual psychological dynamics.

Your motivations for owning a dog will, of course, have a strong effect on the type of dog you choose. Whether you purchase a dog that resembles you or one that compensates for what you lack, your canine selection will confirm the way in which dogs reflect our own self-perceived identities. The hole your dog fills in your life will influence the way you treat her, directly altering her behavior. A dog who is parented will act very differently, for example, than a dog who functions as a therapist. While both have a wealth of poor behaviors simmering just beneath the furry surface, the baby substitute may excel at separation anxiety while the therapist growls at anyone who wants to climb into your bed. By identifying what kind of dog owner you are, you'll uncover the behaviors you will most successfully encourage in your IBD. In this chapter, we'll help you determine:

- Whether your dog plays the role of child, fashion accessory, household fixture, replacement human, narcissistic

extension of self, compensation for inadequacy, or therapist.

- How you will treat your dog according
  to her role.

- Which poor behaviors can be nurtured
  from which types.

- Why refusing to neuter your dog can
  reflect positively on you.

Dog as Child

The recent social shift from dog-as-pet to
dog-as-child is pervasive. With the increasing delay in childbearing, often well into
one's 30s, many individuals bridge the gap
between responsibility-free singlehood and
devoted parenthood with a dog. Those who
never have children continue to relate to
their pets as offspring, while those who do

eventually have kids will one day view their formerly beloved canine child as a nuisance. Dog owners these days refer to themselves as "mommy" or "daddy," and chain pet-supply retailers have begun to advertise their dog products for "pet parents." In fact, whole industries have been built on this phenomenon, from doggy daycare to pet camp to canine psychotherapy.

If you view your dog as a child, you'll spend inordinate amounts of time discussing the social problems, health, and quirky behaviors of your little darling with colleagues and friends, just as you would with a challenging child. You'll speak baby-talk to your little one, make sure your pup is comfortable under her blanket, and worry when she seems a bit down at the snout. You'll have pictures in your wallet or cell phone to show to anyone who's interested. You'll

Doggy Stats

Whether or not IBDs, we love our dogs. From coast to coast, here's how we feel:

- Dogs live in 44.8 million homes in the United States, 40 percent of all households.
- Average annual spending per dog is around $1,500.
- 87 percent of pet owners view their pets as family members.
- 37 percent of pet owners carry pictures of their pets in their wallets.
- 33 percent of dog owners call home to talk to their dogs through the answering machine.
- 57 percent of pet owners would choose their pet as their only companion on a desert island.
- 31 percent of owners have taken off work when their pets are sick.
- 79 percent of pets sleep in their owners' beds.
- 20 percent of pet owners have ended a romantic relationship over a pet.
- 87 percent of owners travel with their dogs.
- 47 percent of pet owners purchase over 10 pet gifts a year; 79 percent give their pets holiday and birthday presents.
- 21 percent of dog owners dress their pets.

worry about the possibility of her death and bemoan the fact that her lifespan is so much shorter than yours.

Treating your dog as a surrogate child offers up many possibilities for IBD behavior. Your dog will be allowed on the furniture, in your bed, and will often run errands with you, thus producing a tantalizing blend of "dog in charge" attitudes with separation-anxiety neuroses. If you're in a couple, you will direct your affection away from your partner and toward the dog, instilling in the dog a sense of dominance and entitlement. Attempts to provide a social life for your dog, whether play dates, doggy daycare, or the dog park, will afford rich opportunities to develop poor dog-on-dog habits. Because children don't need to be walked, it's likely that you'll under-exercise your dog but attempt to make up for it with love, creating poor behaviors related to inactivity. Best of all, you'll be able to see which of your non-dog-loving friends care enough to hear about your sweetheart's endless list of accomplishments and travails.

Dog as Fashion Accessory

Admit it—you dress to get as much attention as possible. When you have an IBD in your purse, you *will* be noticed. After all, a really cute necklace or a shiny belt buckle doesn't pee on clothing displays, yap at Starbucks patrons, or nip valets. You know that every fashionista needs the latest accessories. The newest trend isn't stirrup pants or feather earrings—it's a teensy-weensy dog, preferably to match your outfits. The dog-as-fashion-accessory owner is easy to identify: if you love to shop, take an hour every day to choose your outfits, and regularly max out your credit cards, you know that a toy-sized companion is every season's true must-have.

Accessory dogs are prone to similar types of poor behavior as child dogs. Because they spend all their time with their human, they often manifest separation anxiety. With no exercise, they exhibit neurotic behaviors arising out of boredom and inactivity. They are gloriously demanding and can become territorial, snapping at strangers who attempt to traverse the purse wall.

On the other hand, many fashion-motivated dog owners will pay no more attention to their pets than they would their shoes. When humans treat dogs as inanimate objects, without needs or emotions, the dogs are inclined to manifest all kinds of fabulous attention-seeking neuroses.

> ## Canine Quip
>
> "Why, that dog is practically a Phi Beta Kappa. She can sit up and beg, and she can give her paw— I don't say she will, but she can."
>
> —Dorothy Parker

Dog as Household Fixture

Like the dog-as-fashion-accessory, the main purpose of the dog-as-household-fixture is to complete the owners' sense of what home life should be. Regardless of whether the owners have time or space for a dog, they feel that a dog will complete their household in some way. These are also the individuals who are likely to have 2.4 children because "It's just what you do."

When choosing a dog to match one's home, breed characteristics are secondary to the aesthetic and image needs of the owners.

As you will see in chapter 3, some of the best ill behaviors arise when a dog is selected for reasons other than its behavior and activity needs.

Dogs-as-household-fixture tend to have problems stemming from neglect and inappropriate environment. Whether the dog has high exercise needs and lives in an apartment or has a strong social drive but stays alone all day, you're certain to find multiple poor behaviors to cultivate when a dog suits your interior design and self-image but not your actual lifestyle.

Dog as Replacement Human

Dogs can be the best companions with whom to share emotional challenges. Over millennia, dogs have provided poignant support for those seeking solace. Owners who suffer from anxiety, depression, or neuroses often find that a dog helps them feel better. Rather than relying on friends, family, or a therapist, adopting a dog as your confidante can result in a host of hyper-attachment canine behaviors.

For some owners, the issue is one of trust. Many a woman has muttered, "A dog is better than a boyfriend," while men and country songs tend to claim that dogs are the only mammals who won't do them wrong. Certain dog-acquiring individuals are motivated by great loss, such as the death of a loved one or a hard breakup. Still others just aren't very good at relating to people and thus prefer to make the unconditional, nonverbal love of canines the center of their universe.

Relating to your dog as a substitute human leads to the interpretation of dog behavior in terms of seemingly equivalent Homo sapiens expressions, also known as anthropomorphization. These misunderstandings can produce fantastically poor behavior. In addition, like the dog-as-child and dog-as-fashion-accessory, the dog-as-replacement-human is likely to dominate your household. Due to the intense bond you've probably

The IBD Fixer-Upper

If your IBD isn't exactly the dog you thought she'd be, not to worry—plastic surgery is finally being offered to the underserved canine community, including these procedures:

- Botox injections for inverted eyelashes.

- More attractive drooping for floppy ears.

- Straightening for floppy ears.

- Nose jobs for pugs, bulldogs, and Boston terriers.

- Elimination of unsightly and unhygienic facial or vaginal folds.

- Chin lifts to control drooling.

fostered with your dog, she's sure to mirror your problems. Best of all, the closer you are to your dog, the less you'll have to interact with the outside world, thus increasing your own level of neurosis as well as your dog's.

Dog as Narcissistic Extension of Self

Just like the famous scene in *Lady and the Tramp*, dogs who resemble their owners are no accident. Some people choose dogs to mirror themselves back to them in an endless loop of self-love. This process is largely unconscious. Studies have found that owners of purebred dogs are easily matched to their pets by appearance; this correlation does not exist, however, in mixed-breed dogs whose adult appearance could not be predicted at the time of adoption. This evidence refutes the idea that pet-owner resemblance occurs over time, but instead results from the owner's deliberate choice of dog.

If you choose a dog because it's an extension of your own personality, you're likely to have a dog who will mirror your own behavior. If you're masculine and aggressive, your dog will be, too. Gregarious and outgoing? Exceptionally beautiful and ditzy? Ditto. The great thing about this connection is your dog will also share your flaws and poor behaviors, whether or not you identify them as such.

Dog as Compensation for Inadequacy

When people choose dogs to represent traits they themselves do not possess, the dynamic is almost directly opposite to that of dog-as-narcissistic-extension-of-self. Rather than selecting a dog for what is seen in the mirror, the dog instead reflects what is *not* seen, at least in the owner's eyes.

This type most frequently occurs among men who are insecure about their masculinity, whether psychological or anatomical, and compensate by getting tough, aggressive dogs. In this sounds like you, do not neuter your dog. Who cares about canine overpopulation? You want your dog to display his physical equipment so that everyone will think it represents yours. The more insecure you feel, the meaner-looking dog you will get, not to mention that you will actively cultivate problematic aggressive behaviors to your heart's content so that onlookers will believe you yourself are the tough one (see chapter 9, "Try These at Home").

When women compensate for inadequacy with dogs, they frequently find themselves in the show ring with hyper-feminine

The Castration Conspiracy

As the owner of a male dog, everywhere you turn someone will be urging you to have him neutered. They'll tell you that 6 to 8 million animals enter American shelters every year, of which 3 to 4 million are euthanized. But what does that mean for your IBD—and, more to the point, you?

Your IBD won't be able to fulfill his natural instincts to be aggressive, escape your yard, enjoy sex, and spread his seed. You will have to wince every time you think about or discuss "neutering," which is just another word for castration, something you yourself greatly fear. As the owner of a *male* IBD, you know you won't have to deal with the puppies, anyway.

Most importantly, a neutered dog would not reflect well on your masculinity, something Illinois lawmakers well know. In 2007, the state passed an anti-IBD law that prohibits felons from owning unneutered dogs, claiming that studies show that people with aggressive or vicious dogs tend to have participated in other illegal activity.

If the pro-castration lobby does get to you, there's one last option: Neuticles, testicular implants for dogs. With custom sizing, you can go as big as you like!

breeds. Rather than grooming themselves, these women obsessively groom their pets. The hope is that if the dogs are beautiful enough, no one will notice the women. These dogs tend to exhibit poor behavior associating with entitlement and boredom.

Your Type, Your Dog

In any pursuit, success is more likely when you go with the grain rather than against it. Why start from a position of deficit when cultivating an IBD? Instead, choose the dog and the approach that suit your individual needs. Of course, when reviewing the ownership types and determining which one best describes you, you're bound to notice that there is overlap. These types are not mutually exclusive; instead, they're tendencies that prove useful in determining one's pet psychology. The point of this section

> ## Doggy Dictionary: Furkid
>
> If you think of your dog as your child, refer to your IBD as your "furkid," "furbaby," or "furchild."

is utility, so if you share characteristics of both the dog-as-fashion-accessory and dog-as-child, by all means, avail yourself of both sets of poor behaviors!

If you already have a dog, you've no doubt already instilled some fantastic poor behaviors in your pet. If you haven't yet made your choice, however, the next chapter will help you determine which dog is right for you. As many of these types suggest, the most important factor in selecting a potential IBD is making sure that your decision is based on nothing whatsoever having to do with the dog. Sound complicated? Read on and it will all become clear.

CHAPTER 3
PICKING OUT YOUR DOG: THE RIGHT I.B.D. CHOICE FOR YOU

DOGS ARE THE MOST DIVERSE species on the planet, with more breed varieties than any other animal. Thanks to this plenty, it's hard to go wrong when choosing a dog for poor behavior, so if you made your choice before committing to the IBD way of life, don't worry, because in subsequent chapters we'll discuss ways to maximize any dog's antics. If you do adopt your pet with the cultivation of poor behavior in mind, however, you can select for traits and tendencies that will make your job significantly easier.

For those who prefer less study and work, there is an intuitive way to adopt a dog with a high likelihood for creating chaos. As mentioned in chapter 2, if you choose your dog based not on his temperament but instead on what he looks like and whether he reflects well on you, you'll generally wind up with excellent misbehavior. For this route, don't read up on your prospective dog's breed, don't worry about where he comes from, and don't question whether he fits your lifestyle; instead, just get him because he's cute, exotic, manly, or whatever else floats your boat.

To go about the selection process more deliberately, however, whether you're getting your first, second, or even third dog, you'll want to absorb the intricacies of breed, source, and behavioral tendencies. In this chapter, you'll learn:

- How to match your home environment to your new pet.

- Whether you want a purebred, a designer mixed breed, or a mutt.

- Where to acquire your dog: pet stores and puppy mills vs. animal shelters.

- Why you should get more than one dog.

Choosing the Best Dog for Your Home

When adopting a dog, you'll want to consider both your physical home environment and your household's lifestyle. If you live in a one-bedroom apartment without a yard, for example, opt for a dog with high exercise needs so you can focus his energy on a host of destructive tendencies. A herding dog such as a border collie requires lots of mental stimulation, so this is the perfect match for someone who's rarely at home. While you're out, your border collie will

IBD Naming Protocols

	Male	Female
1	Max	Maggie
2	Jake	Bear
3	Buddy	Molly
4	Bear	Shadow
5	Bailey	Lady
6	Shadow	Sadie
7	Sam	Lucky
8	Lucky	Lucy
9	Rocky	Daisy
10	Buster	Brandy

When you choose a name for your IBD, you could choose a fancy American Kennel Club (AKC) name such as "Champion Gold Mine Diamond Precious Tam O'Shanter," which your dog will never learn. Or, pick from among the most popular monikers. When you go to a busy park and call your dog, any number of dogs will become confused and ill-behaved!

have plenty of time to explore your personal possessions. A dog such as a terrier, bred for hunting small game, will shine in a household full of cats. When considering buying a dog for a young child, take size into consideration. A large, overwhelmingly strong breed such as a rottweiler, Doberman, or chow chow makes an excellent choice to dominate a young child.

Selecting Dog Characteristics

No matter what breeding route you decide to go, there are a few traits to look out for when selecting your dog at a breeder, pet store, or animal shelter. Before choosing, watch the dogs as they interact both with other dogs and with humans, and try to spot the following to make your choice:

- Sensitive to being touched or handled.

- Cringe in response to human contact.

- Extremely high level of activity.

- Aggressive to other dogs; bullying.

- Incessant barking or yapping.

- Pacing.

- Cowering in the corner.

- Obsessive paw licking.

In addition to observable activity, when you talk to the people from whom you are adopting, keep your ears open for dogs that are described as "protective." If a dog has a history of being in multiple homes, you can practically bet on a wide range of poor behavior. Finally, a dog with a "Caution" sign on his kennel is always a great choice. By keeping your eyes open and your intuition keen, you'll no doubt spot the seeds of poor behavior to start your journey.

Purebred, Hybrid, or Mutt?

It is said that there's no such thing as a bad dog, only a bad owner. When it comes to the IBD, we make a subtle modification: there's no such thing as a well-behaved dog, only a bad owner. Thinking in this way will prove liberating as you agonize over which pet to adopt. It's true that selecting for certain characteristics will indeed simplify the process of instilling IBD behaviors, but if you are diligent and skilled in your approach, you will be able to turn any good dog bad. That said, there are some tendencies to consider when choosing your adoption approach.

- **Purebreds:** With purebreds, you can bank on known tendencies arising from centuries of breeding for particular purposes. If you really want to excel with an IBD, purebreds are the safest choice, especially if you go with an unreputable breeder, pet store, or puppy mill (see below).

- **Hybrids:** Hybrids are deliberately mated purebreds, an increasingly popular trend of late. For example, the Labrador retriever plus the poodle creates the Labradoodle, originally combined to create hypoallergenic guide dogs, while the puggle (pug plus beagle) is just plain cute. Until a type of dog "breeds true," meaning two individuals of the same breed consistently produce offspring typical of that breed, it is considered a mixed breed or hybrid. While these dogs are intended to reflect the desired traits of each breed, fortunately for the IBD lover, this plan often works in just the opposite way. Weimardoodles, for example, can often exhibit the neurotic and clingy traits of the Weimaraner along with the intelligence and stubbornness of the poodle. When choosing

IBD Hall of Fame: Chihuahua Attack

In 2005, a pack of angry Chihuahuas attacked a police officer in Fremont, California. After escorting a teenager home from a traffic stop, the officer was charged by five Chihuahuas at the boy's front door. The dedicated public servant sustained multiple bites to his ankles and was treated at a local hospital.

a mixed-breed IBD, be sure to research the character traits of each of the pure-bred ingredients in order to maximize the potential for poor behavior.

- **Mutts:** When you adopt a dog about whom you know nothing of its lineage, you're flying blind with respect to ill behavior. For all you know, your new pet could turn out to be the most mellow, obedient dog of all time. For that reason, purebreds continue to be the most assured route to the IBD. However, if you have a mutt already or believe in rescuing an unwanted animal, with the help of this book, you'll be able to nurture frenzy and lack of control in any dog. You can increase your IBD odds by adopting with any eye toward certain characteristics, however, as outlined further below.

The Purebred IBD

When choosing the breed for your new IBD, there's no shortage of expertise to rely upon. With many years of selective breeding and behavior observation, you can be relatively certain to adopt a dog with the advertised traits. It's especially important with purebreds to buy from pet stores or industrial breeders, as outlined further below.

The Most Popular Breeds— How Do They Stack Up for IBD?		
Breed	**Rating**	**IBD Characteristics**
Border collie	☻☻☻☻☻	Prone to all sorts of neurotic behavior when living in homes without sheep. Intelligence leads to unparalleled invention of never-before-seen ill behaviors.
Chihuahua	☻☻☻☻☻	Extremely prone to aggression. Can be antisocial and high-strung. Frequent yippish barking.
Jack Russell terrier	☻☻☻☻☻	High prey and dominance drives. High activity level. Frequently obnoxious. Requires little work to create IBD.
Weimaraner	☻☻☻☻☻	Extremely neurotic: separation anxiety, destructiveness, obsessive tendencies, and overall anxiety. High activity level.
Boxer	☻☻☻☻	High prey and defensive drives due to former police-dog role. Quick to develop neurotic behaviors like separation anxiety.
Cocker spaniel	☻☻☻☻	Due to 1950s popularity, often inbred and prone to snappy, dominance-related aggression problems combined with timidity, known as "shy-sharp." Puppy-mill dogs prone to wide array of neuroses.

The Most Popular Breeds— How Do They Stack Up for IBD?		
Breed	**Rating**	**IBD Characteristics**
Yorkshire terrier (Yorkie)	🐾🐾🐾🐾	Bossy, yappy, stubborn, and notorious for lack of housebreaking skill.
Beagle	🐾🐾🐾	Generally placid and docile. Can be encouraged to howl. Strong pack drive can lead to separation anxiety. Wanderlust. Puppy-mill breeding produces snappiness.
Doberman pinscher	🐾🐾🐾	High prey, high arousal, and high defense drives, but intelligence and intuition mean that hard work is required to produce Doberman IBD.
Golden retriever	🐾🐾🐾	With high food and social drives, can produce good IBDs as long as not accidentally encouraged to behave. Particularly adept at pulling on leashes and leaping on strangers.
German shepherd	🐾🐾	Well-bred specimens make for poor IBDs, so avoid unless from poor breeding stock, which will result in high defensiveness and aggression fueled by intelligence.
Labrador retriever	🐾🐾	Sadly, most popular dog in America. Bred to be submissive and well-behaved. Choose from hunting rather than show lines due to greater energy and higher arousal levels.

Hybrids: Worst of Both

Designer mixed breeds are the hottest new trend. The American Canine Hybrid Club, established in 1969, lists almost 450 crosses ranging from the affenpoo (*affen*pinscher + *poo*dle) to the zuchon (shih t*zu* + bi*chon* frise). The *-oodle* mixes in particular offer up endless genetically predisposed IBD possibilities. Here are some crosses to consider:

- **Morkie:** *M*altese + *Y*orkie. Definitely a good choice for the accessory-conscious, this hybrid incorporates the flightiness of Yorkshire terriers with the fleecy, easily tangled hair of the Maltese. Both are high-strung, yippy breeds, so IBD possibilities are doubled.

- **Chiranian:** *Chi*huahua + Pom*eranian*. A fantastic choice for the IBD aficionado, this dog retains all the desirable IBD traits of the Chihuahua (aggressiveness, inbreeding) and throws in the belligerence and dominance of the Pomeranian.

- **Borderstaffy:** *Border* collie + *Staff*ordshire terrier. What could be better than a pit bull who's really, really smart?

Puppy Mills and Pet Stores: Your Best Resources

Pet stores almost always have suitable candidates for an IBD because these puppies are almost always purchased in bulk from puppy mills—breeding facilities in which care and socialization with humans are kept to an absolute minimum during the most important imprinting phase of puppy development, five to six weeks of age. Additionally, puppy mills are not rigorous about their breeding protocol, so the likelihood of recessive genes that can contribute to poor behavior is increased.

Try to patronize pet stores that avoid questions about where they buy their puppies or those staffed by teenagers who know nothing about the dogs' origins. Or, you can bypass pet stores entirely. Puppy mills now advertise online and will ship your new dog directly to you.

Above all, avoid breeders who seem knowledgeable about and caring toward their dogs, especially those who quiz you extensively about what kind of home you want to provide. Instead, go with the breeder who wants to make a quick buck.

Animal Shelters and Rescues

The IBD seeker has to be especially careful when it comes to humane societies and the like, as one can easily wind up adopting a well-behaved, mellow dog. The only reason for an IBD lover to visit an animal shelter is in the hopes of rescuing a dog who already exhibits characteristics of poor behavior, anxieties, or phobias. Try in particular for young, active dogs from one to three years old. These dogs have often landed in the shelters because they exhibited a host of behavior problems after outgrowing their cute puppy qualities.

One distinct advantage to adopting an older dog is that you will often know nothing about its prior experiences or upbringing. Dogs who have been in rescue for a long time often develop unique behaviors that would be nearly impossible for you to instill without a considerable investment of hard work.

Multiple-Dog Households

If you already own one dog, consider getting another, because double-dogging can be a great shortcut to ill behavior. Two dogs in a household will play off the tendencies of each other, so that a dog who isn't a barker, for example, will soon become one by mimicking his housemate. A dog who constantly has accidents in the house will soon teach his buddy that this is acceptable (and, in fact, preferable), while a dog that has phobias or separation anxiety will often transfer his neuroses. Essentially, you will get two IBDs without your having to lift a

Truth in Advertising

When deciding which dog to choose from an animal shelter, learn the secret meanings behind the words on the dog's information card.

What It Says	What It Means
"Great guard dog."	Aggressive toward anyone who enters your house, whether friend or foe.
"Shy with strangers."	Poorly socialized—will bite or growl at new people.
"Needs an owner who's home a lot."	Cannot be left alone or he will destroy everything in sight.
"Wants to be an only dog."	Will eat other pets.
"Likes to be in charge."	Tendency to control its owner with aggression.
"Needs experienced owner."	Multiple poor behaviors pre-instilled!
"Shepherd mix."	Pit bull.
"Staffordshire terrier."	Pit bull.
"Amstaff."	Pit bull.

treat. And, if either dog has a propensity for dominance, soon enough they'll *both* dominate you and your house will truly be run by IBDs. As you can imagine, three—or four—is even better.

Let the IBD Begin!

Congratulations on your choice of canine companion, whatever it is. Remember—even if your dog doesn't fit any of the characteristics or breeds outlined above, this book will show you how to transform him into an IBD. In order to nurture your dog, you first need to understand him. Canine behavior reaches back into history even before domestication in the form of primal, instinctual drives. Once you understand these deep motivations and determine which exist in your unique dog, outlined in the next chapter, you'll be able to move toward actual IBD activities.

CHAPTER 4

WHAT DO THEY REALLY WANT? UNDERSTANDING YOUR I.B.D.'S DRIVES

WHILE THE MALLEABILITY OF DOG behavior is one of the features that makes them so appealing to us, and they are capable of learning many of the lessons we teach them, our beloved animals come to us hardwired for various tendencies and instincts. These basic, inborn characteristics are called "drives," some arising from years of selective breeding, a few common to all dogs in varying degrees, and others merely the luck of the genetic draw. In the course of cultivating your IBD, you may be able to modify the expression of your dog's drives, but the drives will never go away. Rather than fighting these drives, you want to harness them to foster poor behavior that goes with your dog's individual character. Just as you learned in chapter 2 to identify your own dog-owning type, so now will you determine your dog's inherent inclinations and then choose behaviors that naturally complement your dog's personality. In so doing you will fully maximize the opportunities for success and make the process fun and rewarding for both you and your IBD. In this chapter, we'll demonstrate:

- What your dog *really* wants from you.

- Why your dog jumps on strangers.

- How to distinguish between the hunt drive and the prey drive.

- What ill behaviors the dominant dog will most likely exhibit.

Dogs and Humans: A Short History of Codependence

To best understand your dog's potential for misbehavior, it's helpful to understand the canine-human relationship. Since Homo sapiens took control of fire, as the story goes, dogs have been best friends, faithful guardians, tireless workers. Or have they? We'd like to think that dogs love us and seek altruistically to please us, but it's more accurate to say that dogs *need* us. Humans and dogs live in a tightly woven web of codependence. From the war mastiffs of ancient Greece to the toy dogs of Victorian society, dogs have protected, amused, and served us. In return, they've received food, shelter, and affection. Throughout, we have selectively bred dogs for certain tasks—inadvertently and fortunately instilling all the necessary ingredients for well-calculated misbehavior.

IBD Hall of Fame: Paw-to-Mouth

Talk about a food drive! For these pooches, mere kibble would never be enough.

British bullmastiff Deefer likes his panties. Or make that women's panties, including thongs; Deefer has expressed no interest in men's underwear. After safely consuming 20 pairs in a year, 3 particularly frilly pairs lodged in his intestines and had to be removed surgically. Fortunately, his family, aware of his habit, had previously invested in pet insurance.

Upon realizing that two $100 bills had disappeared from her coat pocket, a Pennsylvania woman had no idea who the culprit might be—until she cleaned up after her Doberman pinscher, Mia, and found telltale pieces of green paper. Over 24 hours, this proud owner removed the bits of bills from Mia's every poop, then exchanged the remnants for fresh money at her local bank.

Another Brit, Lulu the Labrador, became a suspect when her owner's expensive Gucci watch went missing. An x-ray located the watch, still ticking, and after a quick operation the watch (functional, albeit slightly damaged by stomach acid) was recovered along with a missing sock.

Your Dog Is Driven to Exploit You

Every species evolves to maximize opportunities for survival, and your cute, loving shih tzu is no different. Society has perpetuated the belief that dogs are kind, loving animals whose only joy in life is to satisfy humans and lavish us with unconditional love. While this is a more pleasurable scenario to imagine, in fact your sweet pup is trying to exploit you so that she gets what *she* wants. After you get over the initial hurt of this concept, there's some good news: by understanding this dynamic, it becomes simple to nurture the perfect IBD.

Dogs are hard-wired to extract as many resources from us as possible. Food, water, and shelter are the basics, but these days the spoils of domesticity include top-notch medical care, expensive organic diets, plush bedding, art-quality chew toys, and doting care at luxury kennels. All they have to do in return is make us believe that they love us—and, of course, misbehave.

How did this species exploit us so obviously and yet so insidiously? Easy. First, wild dogs and wolves who weren't fearful of humans—often runts abandoned by their packs—crawled up to us at the campfire to beg for scraps and crumbs, manifesting submissive obeisance. Over time, as shown by the Russian scientist Dmitri Belyaev, the interbreeding of these self-selected canines resulted in surprising genetic shifts. They wagged their tails and licked humans to demonstrate affection. Their ears became floppy, their tails curled, and their coats acquired spots. In all, they became cute.

Dogs have the unique ability to watch us carefully and intuit our desires. We've been misguided for generations into believing that dogs want to please because they convince us—on a daily basis—of their absolute love and affection. What dogs are really looking for, however, is actually primordially selfish: shelter and safety, good meals, successful hunts, power and control over others, and social companionship. Luckily, all these desires can be harnessed to create the ill behaviors we want to foster in the IBD.

One aspect of IBD behavior, as outlined in chapter 1, is canine freedom of choice—allowing your dog to express her innate dogness, released from the constraints of the expectations for the modern dog. Drives are a significant aspect of the authentic inner-dog that you will allow to reemerge.

Like a Michelangelo pulling David out of the block of marble, so will you provide the freedom for your dog to become who she really is.

Understanding Drives

Inherited drives dictate a dog's personality because they define what is intrinsically satisfying to her. Drives are even more influential than intelligence, which for dogs is generally characterized as problem-solving ability. Understanding the seven drives that come into play with dogs will equip you to identify your dog's strengths and weaknesses when it comes to poor behaviors so that you can point her in the right direction.

Drive	Definition	Manifestation	Associated IBD Behavior
Food Drive	Desire to eat.	Snacking, ingesting kibble.	Stealing food.
Sex Drive	Desire to copulate. (Eliminated in spayed or neutered dogs.)	Trying to have sex with other dogs.	Escaping to hunt down the ladies.
Prey Drive	Desire to chase and kill prey.	Chasing small furry animals and shaking them violently after felling them.	Chasing cars.
Defense Drive	Desire to protect self, pack, and territory.	Barking, growling, snapping at, and biting real and imagined threats.	Biting the mailman.
Hunt Drive	Desire to look for prey when it is out of sight.	Relentlessly searching for lost objects.	Obsessive-compulsive tendencies.
Social Drive	Desire for social acceptance and harmony.	Gregarious behaviors, excessive tail wagging, need to be with others.	Jumping on strangers, separation anxiety.
Dominance Drive	Desire to dominate other pack members.	Throwing down other dogs and forcing them to submit. Fighting. Guarding food and other valued objects.	Aggression around the food dish.

What Motivates Your Dog? Bringing Out the Worst

To make it as easy and satisfying as possible for your dog to learn and enjoy ill behaviors, you'll need to observe your pet and find out what makes her tick. Most dogs display tendencies toward one drive over others. Identifying that dominant drive will make it easier to train poor behaviors that are associated with that drive. For example, a dog with a high social drive will want to be around other social beings (human or canine) more than anything else. For this dog, effusive greeting behaviors that manifest themselves as hyperactivity and jumping up are easy to encourage. A dog with a low prey drive but a high defensive drive would make a poor candidate for a cat-chaser but could very easily be encouraged to become an ankle-biter. Once you have identified the your dog's dominant drives, you can begin to think about ways to nurture them and set your dog up for IBD success.

Food Dog

A dog with a high food drive will:

- Seek out food to the exclusion of all other outside stimuli.

- Drool incessantly when presented with the opportunity to eat.

- Wolf down food—it's all good.

- Snap at the hand that feeds her, in order to swallow food more quickly.

- Respond quickly to any visible treat, and often present different behaviors (sitting, rolling over, barking) to try to generate more morsels.

- Eat to excess, often displaying obesity if food intake is not carefully monitored.

Of course, all dogs have the food drive, but some dogs focus on food with undistractable intent. If your dog is a food dog, she will succeed

---

IBD Indigestion

Pica, an endlessly entertaining dog neurosis, is the propensity for ingesting inedibles, including the following documented objects that required medical treatment:

Battery*	Golf ball*	Plastic chicken
Cell phone	Hearing aid	Pool ball
Cigarette lighter	iPod*	Razorblade
Condom*	Kebob skewer*	Scissors
Diaper*	Magnet	Tampon*
Fake excrement	Marijuana	Vibrator*
Glass eye*	Metal fork	Videotape

*Multiple items swallowed by the same dog.

---

at begging, stealing food, counter-
surfing, and foraging.

Sex Dog

A dog with a high sex drive will:

- Hump other dogs.

- Hump inanimate objects such as
  stuffed animals.

- Hump legs.

- Whine or cry when in the presence
  of female dogs in heat.

- Show aggression toward other
  male dogs but not necessarily
  female ones.

If your male dog is intact (not neutered; see "Dog as Compensation for
Inadequacy" in chapter 2) then he
will have a naturally high sex drive.

A sexed-out dog will excel at escaping the yard, running away to chase after females, refusing to come when called, and dog-on-dog aggression.

Prey Dog

A dog with a high prey drive will:

- Show a huge interest in small furry objects.

- Show a huge interest in small furry animals.

- Stalk birds.

- Chase cats.

- Chase bicycles, skateboards, and in-line skaters.

- Chase with vigor and glee after tennis balls and other tossed toys.

- Enjoy retrieving.

- Shake and "kill" stuffed toys.

- Instigate games by shoving toys in your lap.

If you have a prey-driven dog, you are one lucky owner. The prey drive leads to all sorts of ill behaviors. Your dog will be a superstar at chasing and killing cats, squirrels, and other small wildlife; chasing cars; dog-on-dog aggression (directed toward smaller dogs); and excessive destruction inside the house. A select group of highly driven prey dogs will develop obsessive fetching behaviors. A prey dog may or may not also have the hunting drive (see below), while the hunting dog will *always* have the prey drive.

Defense Dog

A dog with a high defense drive will:

- Show a distrust of strangers, often cringing from contact.

- Run up to unknown people, nip their ankles or legs, and then immediately retreat.

- Bare her teeth, growl, or snap when backed into a corner, especially by people she doesn't like.

- Bark ferociously at people or dogs when on the leash during walks.

- Bark at passersby while in the car, regardless of their appearance and whether they pose a credible threat to the automobile.

- Guard the house relentlessly, often engaging in diligent perimeter control to make sure security has not been breached.

- Misbehave during visits to the vet or the groomer.

It is incredibly easy to manipulate a highly defensive dog to bring out the worst behaviors; this quality is thus highly desirable in the IBD. A dog who naturally fears and suspects the unknown easily learns to growl at and bite strangers, chase the mail carrier, attack trespassing animals, snap at children, bark incessantly, and develop neurotic behaviors.

Hunt Dog

A dog with a high hunt drive will:

- Unnaturally fixate on tennis balls or other retrievable objects.

- Perceive light beams (from a mirror or flashlight) as prey.

- Search for hours for lizards, squirrels, cats, rodents, or other living creatures that may be inhabiting your backyard.

- Destroy such objects as your couch that stand between her and her toys.

- Stalk birds with incredible stealth and patience.

Hunting dogs tend to focus on lost objects, which leads them to excel at interior home destruction. These noble animals will also exhibit neurotic behaviors, which manifest themselves as self-mutilation, obsessive-compulsive rituals, refusing to come when called, and stand-offishness toward owners. As noted previously, a hunting dog will always have the prey drive as well.

Social Dog

A dog with a high social drive will:

- Love other dogs to excess.

- Enjoy dog parks, doggy daycare, and other social venues more than anything.

- Show enormous amounts of excitement at meeting new people, dogs, and other animals.

- Greet the world vigorously with the notion that all people and dogs will be in their fan club.

- Love to go to the vet or groomer.

- Jump up on anyone that comes to the door.

- Pull on the leash to hail strangers.

Social dogs are the most common dogs today. While it may be difficult to instill certain poor behaviors more typical of the other drives, there are still plenty of social impulses that can be harnessed for chaos. A dog who is highly social craves your attention and affection and therefore succeeds at separation anxiety, effusive greeting, hyperactivity, drooling, jumping up, pulling on the leash, barking, and begging.

Dominance Dog

A dog with a high dominance drive will:

- Bully other dogs for position at the door or food dish.

- Take valued objects or treats from other dogs by growling.

- Will meet and greet other dogs with an upright, stiff posture and a high tail carriage.

- Will physically dominate her owner by pushing or leaning.

- Will guard her own objects against approaching "threats."

Doggy Dictionary: Peternity Leave

When you get your new IBD, make sure you demand "peternity leave," time off from work to bond. Also called "puppy leave."

- Will control her household by using violence—growling, snapping, or biting—to get what she wants.

It's easy to foster IBD behavior in the dominance dog: just be passive and allow the dog to do whatever she wants. A dominant dog is best suited for territorial aggression, biting or snapping at her owner, fighting at the food dish, fighting with other dogs, general disobedience, and pulling on the leash.

The IBD Drive

Now that you've identified the basic drives in your dog, you'll be able to focus on developing the ill behaviors that are associated with your dog's drives, and learning will be faster and more satisfying for both of you.

Bear in mind that all dogs have behaviors associated with all the drives, and most dogs are dominant in more than one drive. The trick is to harness your dog's primary drives and exploit them. With a dog who exhibits the characteristics of many drives, the IBD possibilities are endless.

Now that you know what kind of owner you are, why dogs are the way they are, and what kind of dog you have, it's time to start with actual behavioral modification. In chapter 5, you'll learn how to approach your relationship with your dog, setting up the foundation for IBD development.

CHAPTER 5
ESTABLISHING THE FOUNDATION: THE SIX I.B.D. CORNERSTONES

BEFORE ANY DOG TRICKS OR SPE-cific behaviors are reinforced by human interaction, a relationship is developed between person and pet, with behavior-reaction dynamics that the dog quickly learns to identify. As with any endeavor, when it comes to cultivating an IBD there are short cuts and long detours, easy and labor-intensive approaches. By absorbing the six cornerstones of the IBD philosophy, you will fluidly nurture your IBD in your day-to-day life without spending inordinate amounts of time. If you follow our easy principles, you'll soon find that your dog is *naturally* becoming more and more ill-behaved. In this chapter, you'll learn the secrets to the IBD, including:

- The six cornerstones of the IBD philosophy: dominance permission, inconsistency, confusion, ineffectual repetition, anthropomorphism, and lack of exercise.

- Why consistency is the hobgoblin of little minds.

- Whether it's better for one person or several to cultivate your IBD.

- How to foster complete indifference to commands.

Give Dominance Permission

The sooner you give up your notion of control over your dog, the more success you will have in your IBD quest. This idea is counterintuitive in a society that feels dogs should be subservient to humans, but life is far more interesting when a dog is making the decisions. You'll want to discard any previously held beliefs about household hierarchy and cede control to your dog.

To accomplish this, remind yourself that he is in charge, not you. Because he is the pack leader, he gets first choice as to where he sleeps, what he eats, and when and where he goes out. Your job as owner is to provide him with as many opportunities for dominance as possible. Encourage him to experiment with a variety of dominance behaviors, including jumping all over you, pulling and lunging on the leash, guarding food, and humping. Humping, while often misinterpreted as a sexual behavior, is usually a sign of dominance. The dog is really saying, "Take that!" If your dog shows an interest in humping you, your leg, or your

IBD Insurance

As an IBD owner, you want to make sure that your dog is covered by your homeowner's or renter's insurance. When you're protected from the financial burden of property damage as well as the inevitable, probably well-deserved bite, your dog can run free on his path to destruction while you sit back and enjoy it.

Dog bites are welcome business for insurance companies, accounting for as much as 25 percent of all liability claims and 6 percent of claim costs. More than 4.7 million people are bitten each year; about 20 percent need medical attention. Over half of dog-bite victims are children.

To make sure you're covered, request a $2 million umbrella policy to cover liability for your car and house. This excessive coverage will cost you a bit more, but at least you'll be protected should Fido take a nip out of the mailman.

guests, push him away meekly, being careful not to actually dislodge him. The timid effort will encourage him to be more forceful in his dominance displays, resulting in even more humping.

One common mistake made by novice IBD owners stems from the belief that dogs engage in certain behaviors, such as climbing onto the furniture, out of love or a desire to be near you. Your dog may love you, but first and foremost, he wants to control you and your resources, and you need to make sure you allow that. An excellent way to reinforce your dog's sense of self-importance is allowing him to choose and control where he sleeps. Naturally, he'll choose your bed, and, with any luck, will have you sleeping at the very edge while he takes over the prime central real estate—under the covers, of course. In the case of couples, allow him to sleep in between the two of you.

Other ways to foster dominance include:

- Feeding him before you eat, while you watch.

- Giving in to all demands for food or treats, including limitless samples of your own snacks or meals.

- Allowing him complete access to furniture, throws, and pillows. If he's a small dog, make sure you provide him a way to jump up, such as stacks of books for a makeshift stairway.

- Giving him first choice as to where he hangs out. If you're in his way, move.

- Letting him decide where he goes on his walks, as well as what he sniffs and for how long.

- Allowing him to guard any favorite objects (including other family members); if he growls when you approach, back off.

Practice Inconsistency Inconsistently

Because dogs learn obedience through consistency, this tired approach is the sacred cow of obedience training. Life is more fun, however, with an unpredictable dog. A dog that jumps out of car windows, disappears for days at a time, or rearranges your décor on an ongoing basis is ripe fodder for those little anecdotes we all love to tell, and you'll never be bored. Varied and developed behaviors will spring, almost magically, from inconsistency.

In order to have an unpredictable dog, you must learn to be unpredictable yourself. What's better than never knowing what exciting event awaits you? A dog who is constantly and actively reacting to his environment is happier and more engaged than the obedient dog-drone.

The Miracle of Anthropomorphism

Anthropomorphism—attributing human characteristics to nonhuman animals—is an ideal way to approach your dog. If this were not the case, Cassius Marcellus Coolidge's paintings of dogs playing poker would never have been so popular for over a hundred years.

When you interact with your dog, assume he has emotions and feelings exactly the same as yours. After all, *he* believes that *you* think like a dog. Theories suggest that domesticated animals who don't provide food, labor, or material goods—so-called social parasites—evolved a "cute response" to elicit our parental instincts. Wouldn't it stand to reason that they would also evolve such emotions as guilt, remorse, and jealousy? (Not that IBDs, of course, *should* ever feel these things.)

Aesthetically, dogs are bred specially for their human qualities, with plumes and expressive faces, all the better to be dressed and coddled. Why not interpret their actions as smiles, pouts, or hugs? Or imagine that they understand the passage of time and abstract cause and effect? After all, not only is anthropomorphism easier than interspecies understanding, it's also more effective at eliciting ill behavior.

To avoid accidentally being consistent, follow these tenets:

- Practice inconsistency at all times, but not consistently. Never do the same thing twice, except sometimes. Make sure your dog's day is full of surprises.

- If ever you want your dog to do something specific, vary the command words: "Sit!" could just as easily be phrased as "Fido, take a load off." You can even speak to your dog in different languages. Does it matter that your dog doesn't understand Japanese? Of course not.

- Change the rules as often as you can, then don't enforce them. If he never knows the rules, they're very easy for him to break!

Multi-Layered Confusion

Ideally, several different people will participate in handling your dog. Varied influences will naturally create an aversion in your dog to any particular behavior, injecting his life with a healthy degree of confusion. When your dog is confused, he's much more likely to engage in behaviors that he himself finds fulfilling. You'll want to give him many choices for activities so he can select his own path, as a dog with a vast array of options ("What should I chew *now*?") will undoubtedly choose the most ill-behaved ones.

Consistent with the concept of inconsistency, make sure that every member of your household has different rules and expectations for your dog. By providing your dog with many cues, none of them similar, you avoid accidentally teaching your dog to be obedient. For example, "Come!" might mean "Run in my direction" or it could just as well communicate, "Hey, we're leaving the dog park now, so if you don't want to go, flee in the other direction." Make sure that "Come!" is not being actively enforced in the traditional sense. Once your dog has cleverly avoided a narrow interpretation of a command in favor of a broader—and more optional—one, he will develop his own versions, a great foundation for ill behaviors.

Other commands that lend themselves to multiple interpretations include:

- **"Heel":** Different household members should walk your dog differently—one person with the dog on the right side, one on the left, one with a very long leash, etc. One should allow the dog to sniff, the other should pull him along.

- **"Down":** Because *down* can mean both "Lie down!" and "Stop jumping!" this command is great for families. Use it both ways, inconsistently. Remember, too, that *lie down* can mean, "Put all of your body parts on the ground," "Roll over and recline to the side," or "Roll over on your back and grab the leash in your mouth."

Ineffectual Repetition for Feigned Indifference

Feigned indifference goes hand in hand with inconsistency and is the result of ineffectual repetition. When you repeat something again and again, it loses meaning. If you observe successful IBD owners, you'll see that they repeat to their dogs: "sit-sit-sit-SIT!" Their dogs have already learned that if they don't sit on the first command, nothing happens. If there is no consequence to disobedience then the dog is free to pursue his own interests. Thus the dog pretends he has absolutely no idea what *sit* actually means.

When addressing your dog, therefore, make sure you repeat commands over and over again. Soon "Sit!" will have no more impact on your dog than "Noodles!" Your dog may or may not choose to sit when asked, and this is the thought process to foster when developing an IBD.

You also want to cultivate your dog's feigned indifference to his own name. An

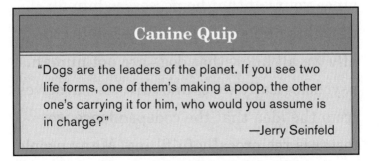

Canine Quip

"Dogs are the leaders of the planet. If you see two life forms, one of them's making a poop, the other one's carrying it for him, who would you assume is in charge?"

—Jerry Seinfeld

obedience-trained dog will, upon hearing his name, swivel his head toward the voice calling him, as if to say, "What?" On the contrary, the correct IBD response is complete ignorance. To cultivate this, repeat the dog's name in such a way that he soon becomes immune to it ("Fido, Fido, Fido, Fido, Fido," followed by no discernible action) or implement a host of nicknames so your dog is never really sure what his name actually is.

Pro-Anthropomorphism

When approaching the IBD, you must convince yourself that he possesses human thoughts and emotions. While intellectually we all know that dogs are not human, psychologically we cannot divorce ourselves from the idea that the codependence we foster is reciprocally fulfilling. Many people truly believe that their dogs empathize on a deeper, human level. Whether or not this is true is irrelevant. The important thing is to treat your dog like a human in order to create a host of behavior problems.

By projecting your own feelings onto your dog, you'll be able to reinterpret standard canine behavior. For example, at least half of the owners of rescued dogs claim their dog was abused. While certainly some dogs have experienced terrible treatment, the cringing that dogs display when voices or hands are raised is a completely normal canine response of submission. Nevertheless, we continue to explicate their behavior as human, and in doing so, we begin to *treat* the dog like a human (an equal or superior, as in the "Give Dominance Permission" section above) as well as misunderstand what the dogs actually need, thus fostering poor behavior.

Other anthropomorphic misinterpretations include:

- **Dogs understand time.** Dogs do not register the passage of time like people do. Believing that your dog misses you more if you're gone longer will result in more effusive displays of affection on your part when you return, thus laying the groundwork for a good case of separation anxiety.

- **Dogs understand democracy.** Dogs work in a strictly hierarchical social system. If there is more than one dog in the household, treating both dogs as equals will successfully blur the status lines between them, leading to squabbling over food, treats, and toys, as well as the development of excessive dominance, which will usually manifest itself in some type of aggression.

Law-Breaking IBDs

There's a small legal industry geared toward restricting the rights of your IBD. From leash laws to pooper-scooper regulations, a small group of anti-dog citizens have imposed their preferences on the rest of us.

Leash laws actually work somewhat in the IBD's favor. Because they feel cornered, dogs tend to be more aggressive when *on* a leash than when allowed to walk freely! Additionally, most dog bites occur on private property, often within the owner's home or yard.

When it comes to pooper-scooper laws, most people would agree that the job of cleaning up 2 million tons of dog feces annually in the United States is better performed by cities and gardeners. Besides—how hard is it to wash off a shoe?

- **Dogs need to engage in sex.** Dogs are often left unneutered because owners believe that their pets need to engage in sexual activity for complete fulfillment. Intact dogs leave the door open for many IBD behaviors, *and* many more IBDs.

- **Dogs don't enjoy regular dog food.**
  Throughout history, dogs have been
  scavengers, eating only leftovers at
  irregular intervals. When a dog is
  believed to be human, food suddenly
  becomes much more important. Owners
  begin to cater to the dog's gustatory
  whims just as they would for a fussy
  child, which results in extremely selective eating habits.

Never Exercise Your Dog

By walking or running your dog, playing
fetch or Frisbee, or hiring a dog walker,
you waste valuable physical and emotional
energy that is better directed toward poor
behavior. A well-exercised dog tends to
lounge about the house doing very little
when he isn't involved in his daily activity—
not a prime example of an IBD, to be sure.

A Solid Foundation
for Poor Behavior

The six pillars on which the IBD philosophy proudly rests will serve you throughout
your IBD journey, no matter which specific
behaviors you choose to cultivate. When
combined with principles of reward and
deterrent, the subject of the next chapter,
these basic principles will allow you to
point your dog in any IBD direction.

CHAPTER 6
REWARDS AND DETERRENTS: ILL-BEHAVIOR MODIFICATION

BASIC BEHAVIOR THEORY WORKS on many species, including spouses. Here, however, we want to apply its tools toward developing a successful IBD. In order to provide the correct responses to your dog, you need to understand how behavior is shaped. These tools are no different from those used in traditional obedience training; they are just applied to different behaviors, and more pleasurably at that.

Behavioral modification is accomplished by a combination of positive reinforcement, which is rewarding a behavior (for example, with food) in order to increase it, and positive punishment (also called negative reinforcement), which is correcting unwanted behavior via an aversive (such as a sharp leash correction) in order to decrease it. Finally, ignoring an unwanted behavior functions to extinguish it.

While it seems a bit theoretical at this point, don't worry—we'll give you the concrete tools you need, including such lessons as:

- Recognizing non-food rewards for your dog.

- Harnessing the power of unpredictability.

- Limiting inadvertent rewards that encourage obedience.

- Using the powerful "jackpot" theory of variable rewards.

Positive Reinforcement to Encourage Poor Behavior

With behavior theory, you want to reward behaviors that you like, because every time you reward a behavior, you increase the likelihood that it will occur again. Dogs generally repeat behaviors that feel good, taste good, or accomplish a goal.

Rewards for your dog aren't confined to food treats. Destruction sessions (ripping apart pillows), freedom (bolting out the door), and prey pursuits (chasing the cat) could be intrinsically rewarding for your dog, depending on her personality. In chapter 4, you identified what motivates your dog, and indeed the key to reinforcing ill behavior is to identify what is of high value for your dog then to provide those items or experiences when she behaves badly.

Reward #1: Things that Feel Good

The number-one reason a dog repeats a behavior is because it feels good to her. This could be a fond pat on the head, but more likely it's something that feels good on a much deeper level. The pursuit of your dog's drives

Retractable Leashes for IBDs

There is no better piece of equipment for the IBD than the retractable leash. This innovation consists of a thin nylon line, generally 15 to 18 feet long, that spring-coils out of a plastic housing. A button provides "brakes."

Retractable leashes give IBDs freedom, a huge radius within which they can eat inappropriate objects, jump on strangers, and attack approaching dogs. The thin nylon line is impossible to grab in urgent situations, nor can you effectively reel it in. Unlike with a standard leash, you don't run the risk of accidentally punishing poor behavior with a collar correction. Finally, retractable leashes cause severe rope burns to bystanders who get in the way of your IBD's high-speed chases.

feel good to her. For example, a social dog will feel best when she's engaged in social interactions, so you'll want to greet her effusively when she jumps on you even if you are simultaneously saying "Off!" in a friendly tone of voice. Keep in mind that some dogs respond quite well to any attention, even what we sometimes call "negative attention"—yelling, pushing, or chasing. These types of responses are often interpreted by your dog as an invitation to play, and thus can be considered a reward for poor behavior.

Reward #2: Things that Taste Good

All dogs can be rewarded with things that taste good. Providing a tidbit or treat (or big juicy steak) will always reinforce a poor behavior.

Reward #3:
Things that Accomplish a Goal

A dog who's trying to achieve something (and remember, what he is trying to achieve depends on his drives) will experiment with different tactics. Whichever tactic is successful will be repeated. For example, if your dog wants to come inside, she will first scratch at the door, then bark, then whine, etc. Reward all of these behaviors by opening the door.

Discouraging Unwanted Behavior

When your dog performs in a way you don't like—for example, if she sits or stays on command—you will want to correct it with an aversive, which is essentially the opposite of a reward. Dogs avoid behaviors that feel bad, are frightening or unpredictable, or don't accomplish goals. Inflicting aversives is no fun, so fortunately they're rarely necessary to attain the IBD, one of the many pleasures of this approach.

Aversive #1: Things that Feel Bad

This is probably the most common method for obedience training. There are many aversive obedience-training products on the market, ranging from choke chains to electric fences. Understandably, dogs don't repeat behaviors that cause them pain or discomfort, but why would you want to cause your dog pain or discomfort?

Aversive #2: Unpredictable Things

Dogs like predictable reactions from everyday objects. Loud, startling noises or sudden movements can be frightening. For example, the sound of a glass breaking or the motion of an umbrella opening terrifies dogs, who don't expect inanimate objects to behave this way. You'll want to be careful to avoid these types of unpredictable situations for two reasons: one, she won't be desensitized to her fears and will become increasingly anxious, possibly phobic; and two, you don't want to discourage certain types of poor behavior. For example, if your dog jumps to retrieve the bacon that's been left on the counter and accidentally sends a platter flying across the floor, shattering noisily into a hundred pieces, she may never eat off the counter again.

Aversive #3:

Things that Don't Accomplish Goals

A dog will soon abandon behaviors that don't accomplish goals. If your

Persuading the Mailman to Leave

Have you ever wondered why dogs seem to hate the mailman? Many believe it's the uniform, but that detail comes after the fact. Here's how it works: mail carriers come every day, around the same time, and invade the property. Due to the incredibly convincing defense mounted by your dog, the carrier leaves. Your dog believes that it's his barking, growling, and spinning that deters the mailman from sticking around—he has no idea that the mailman has to finish his route. Your dog is intelligently repeating behaviors that accomplish a daily goal: get the guy in the funny trousers to leave.

This is no joke to the post office. In 2004, the Canadian pet chain Pet Valu began carrying Bark Bars, dog treats shaped like mail carriers. The Canada Post—which documents some 300 dog attacks per year—protested, and Pet Valu voluntarily pulled the treats.

dog is trying to get you to pet her by nudging your elbow with her nose, and that doesn't work, she'll up the up the ante by squeezing her entire head under your arm, cycling through different tactics until she finds one that works. Rather than ignoring her, which could serve to extinguish the behaviors, you'll want to show her that many different such behaviors will accomplish her desired goals.

Recognizing Inadvertent Rewards and Punishments

Remember those dog owners who, without seeming to lift a finger, have perfect IBDs? Chances are they both increase rewards and limit punishments without any idea that they're doing so. With this in mind, you'll need to be careful that you don't accidentally reward behaviors you don't want reinforced. For example, if you absentmindedly hand your dog a cookie while she's sitting still—or worse, treat her for promptly answering your call to come—she might do it again. You don't want to be faced with an obedient dog, so make sure to reward deliberately.

Recognizing and limiting possible punishments is even trickier. Many ill behaviors are instinctively punished. For example, a dog who bites the postman might get kicked in return, thereby making her cautious of nipping others in the future. A dog who pulls on the leash might receive an unintentional collar correction. Care must be exercised to avoid these potential aversives or your dog may choose to avoid ill behaviors altogether.

The Power of Variable Reward: The "Jackpot" Theory

Ever wonder why the slots in Vegas are so popular? People are lured to them for the possibility of a big reward. They drop in quarter after quarter, hoping to hit it big. Along the way, they're rewarded every so often with a small token, just enough to keep them interested. "If I keep doing this," they think, "sooner or later I'll get the big prize."

Your dog's mind works in the same way. In order to make a behavior really stick, you have to convince your dog that every so often she'll get something fantastically great—if she keeps working at it. In the meantime, you've got to keep her interested with a series of randomly spaced, small rewards until she hits the jackpot. This is called "variable reward" because the intervals between the rewards vary.

The "jackpot" is the be-all and end-all of rewards. Make sure your dog "jackpots" at least once for every poor behavior you are trying to instill, and she'll never forget it. For example, a dog who's been fed once from the table will continue begging for years without results, until one night when the polite but vegetarian Aunt Sally comes to visit and feeds the dog her steak under the table—jackpot!

Reward Yourself with an IBD

It takes some discipline to be sure that you're rewarding the poor behaviors you want and averting the obedience that you don't, but after the initial learning period, you'll be impressed by the extent to which your dog is able to take your shoe and run with it. It all comes down to mindfulness— be aware of the signals you're sending your dog so that you can deliberately shape her poor behavior.

Now that you understand the broad strokes of canine psychology, it's time to start tackling some actual behaviors. In chapter 7, we're going to put your newfound knowledge to work.

CHAPTER 7
BEGINNING I.B.D. SKILLS: NO BOUNDARIES ALLOWED

WELCOME TO THE SECTION OF THE book you probably thought we were going to start with—actual ill behaviors and how to instill them. Hopefully you now see, however, how important it was to cover all the fundamentals. With those tools, even if the bad behaviors we outline aren't the ones you desire, you'll be able to figure out a way to develop those you do seek.

While chapter 8 outlines more advanced behaviors, chapter 7 focuses on the early development of the IBD: boundaries, house-breaking, socialization, and destruction, all rich breeding grounds for poor behavior. Even if you're starting with an adult dog rather than a puppy, you can still backtrack to instill some of these basic behaviors. While we do address failing to come on command and pulling on the leash, of course we don't touch upon such useless "skills" as sitting, staying, etc. Among the many things you will learn in this chapter are:

- Why you should never crate your dog.

- How failing to housebreak will improve your immunity.

- How to transmit your social nervousness to your pup.

- Why to call your dog when he doesn't want to come.

The Myth of the Dog Cave

A particularly nasty myth has circulated among obedience trainers over the last two decades: the idea that dogs like to be crated. These self-proclaimed experts claim that dogs enjoy crates because they are "den-like" and dogs, after all, are den animals. Though it may be difficult to get the dog to use his crate at first, the party line goes, soon enough he'll willingly enter the crate and actually prefer it.

Nothing could be further from the truth. Give any dog the choice of a crate or a down-filled comforter on a Posturepedic with human company and he'll always choose the latter. Who are the crates for, then? Humans! Some owners actually want time apart from their dogs, or want to limit household access, especially if the owners aren't at home.

We're not concerned, however, with *who* desires the crate; our priority is that crating disrupts IBD goals. The best IBDs don't have any boundaries. They go where they want, when they want. All time with humans is "on" time, and the dogs are in charge. Additionally, you don't want to teach your dog to "self-soothe," "be comfortably alone," or "take a time out," as the obedience nonsense states. These dynamics will infringe on your dog's ingenuity and take away from his necessary experience seeking out entertainment in your home. If your dog isn't used to crate-like environments, if he ever does find himself in such a situation, he'll make plenty of noise, the healthy canine reaction.

Finally, crates limit the amount of damage your dog can inflict on your household. Why would you want to do that?

Where There's a Will

Why leave your earthly riches to your IBD? Because pets are considered property, and property can't own property, pets cannot legally inherit money. You can, however, establish a trust to provide the best of care. While there are no national laws around estate planning for pets, 35 states have enacted legislation recognizing their legality. Some one million Americans have designated their pets as beneficiaries, and the average bequest is around $25,000. Some individuals even leave post-death instructions and funds for their pet to be relocated to quasi–retirement communities, luxury resorts where pets can live out the rest of their owner-free days.

Rich dogs are the stuff of both legends and truth; Gunther the Alsatian shepherd's hundreds of millions of dollars, for example, may be apocryphal. Doris Duke left her dog $100,000, while actress Betty White has reportedly willed all to her pets. A British mutt named Jasper controls almost $300,000 and has the run of his own thirteenth-century estate.

With an IBD, you might want to speak to an attorney about protecting your pooch from liability issues—deep pockets and poor behavior may be a bad combination.

Housebreaking Is Overrated

Limiting your dog's elimination habits is not only time-consuming for you, it runs counter to natural canine behavior. In the wild, wolves may not do their business near where they sleep, but everywhere else is fair game. Dogs are no different. They want the freedom to go whenever, wherever. No dog chooses to be housebroken.

If dogs had their druthers, they would mark their territory, which of course consists of your house. (This has the added advantage of preventing strange dogs from approaching your home without trepidation.) Additionally, dogs like to smell the spots where they've previously eliminated, so using the home's interior will provide them with greater entertainment and pleasure than if they were forced to go outside.

Most dog owners only housebreak their dogs because they've been taught that dog waste is filthy and unhygienic. However, recently scientists have shown that exposure to healthy bacteria is actually beneficial in building immunity to illnesses and disease.

If you do choose to housebreak, be sure to practice such ineffective means of reinforcement as rubbing your dog's face in its messes or scolding him after the fact. Those reactions do nothing to further the cause of housebreaking but tend to promote poor behavior, so you may come out ahead after all. And if the clean-up really bothers you, you can always use dog diapers. These are sold in two models: a "belly band" for males and undergarment-style panties for females. As you can imagine, your dog will really enjoy wearing them.

Social Behavior and the IBD

The properly cultivated IBD has many
social behaviors at his disposal, with basic
tendencies depending on his individual
drives. Some IBDs will bite and snap at
strangers, bark excessively, attack other
dogs, and start fights, while others will
jump, nudge, push, sniff, and "say hello"
even if the dog or human he is greeting

IBD Hall of Fame: Elvis's Teddy Bear

One night in 2006, a Doberman pinscher guard
dog called Barney went berserk in a British
children's museum. His target? The collection
of rare teddy bears he was supposed to be
protecting, worth some $900,000, including a
$75,000 bear named Mabel (now beheaded),
that once belonged to Elvis Presley. Theories
on why the dog, not previously characterized as
an IBD, went on such a rampage ranged from
stimulation by the scent of Elvis to jealousy over
the museum staff's affection for Mabel.

would clearly prefer that he not do so. While sociability has some roots in genetics, it is to a large extent fostered by environment. With a few tips, you'll have no trouble developing anti-social behavior in your dog.

Socializing a Puppy

A poorly socialized puppy will turn into a fearful, nervous adult—a truly desirable IBD profile. A dog that has little or no exposure to new sounds, new scents, and new sights, not to mention new people and other dogs, will naturally have a higher defensive drive than a dog who's been paraded all over town. The high defense drive is critical in developing barking, growling, and snapping behaviors.

Dogs also pick up on the emotions of their owners. When with your dog, be fearful as others approach. Pull him off to the side or pick him up to let them pass. When he growls or cowers, pet him to reinforce his behavior (make it look like you are just soothing him). If he barks and lunges, get down to his level and say "There, there" as you stroke his brow, as if calming him down. With this kind of positive reinforcement, he'll repeat these behaviors in no time!

On the other hand, if your dog has a high social drive, you'll want to encourage this enviable lack of boundaries. Dogs greet one another by jumping up, mouthing and licking at each other's faces, and running around excitedly, yapping and barking. These are natural behaviors, which become even more charming in full-grown dogs. If you have a puppy, make sure that you don't accidentally discourage these greeting rituals with harsh words, leash corrections, or refusing to pay attention. Instead, receive your dog warmly and enthusiastically when he jumps onto your best suit when you come home from work, or pretend to swat him away, murmuring "No" and his name so he can enjoy that game. When guests come to visit, don't put your dog into a sit-stay when they arrive. He's your best ambassador, so let him loose!

Dog-on-Dog Etiquette

Places such as the dog park provide excellent environments for instilling poor social behavior in your dog. When teaching your dog how to play with others, you can go in one of two ways: turning your dog into a sissy or a bully.

Creating a bully can start with young puppies. From the time they can walk, puppies engage in play fighting. These behaviors establish dominance, teach bite inhibition, and encourage good social skills, whereby a dog learns how to avoid fights by exhibiting the proper cues of dominance and submission. With exposure to properly socialized dogs, your puppy learns how to control his play and limits the damage that might result from rough play. Because this is not your goal as the owner of the IBD, you'll need to counter-condition your pup to play rough. To do this, pair him with an older, larger dog that will bully him (active dogs in the 12-to-18-month-old range are a good choice) then let them roughhouse. If a fight ensues, don't break it up; instead, let them hash it out and learn that fighting solves every squabble. Cheering your dog on will further cement this behavior.

On the other hand, if your dog is timid and you are a nervous Nellie, you will want to interfere in his play in order to inhibit his social skills. While dogs growl and vocalize even during the friendliest of wrestling matches, assume that every sound is a sign that your precious pooch is about to be killed. Jump in prematurely and call his name repeatedly, then pull him away from the other dogs. When he attempts to return to his buddies, start the process over again.

Walking the Human

Walking nicely on a leash—or heeling, as it's sometimes called—is one of more difficult behaviors to properly obedience-train. It's therefore no surprise that one the easiest behaviors to cultivate is walking *poorly* on a leash. After all, most dogs do it naturally. They are far more interested in what's going on around them than they are in keeping pace with your stride. Bugs, grass, birds, squirrels—the entire great outdoors offers up myriad sniffing opportunities, and your dog should be encouraged to investigate them all, for however long he wants.

The most important thing to remember on walks is that your dog is in charge, not you. He chooses the direction, speed, and intensity. From the very beginning of the excursion, he should lead the way, walking through doors and gates before you. Even if you began your jaunt with the intention of walking to Starbucks, let him choose the path. He'll soon lead you to fascinating places you'd never see on your own, like alleyways, garbage piles, and gutters. Along the way, make sure that he's allowed to greet in his own fashion whatever traffic you may encounter. Whether he is aggressive or effusive, part of the joy of a daily walk lies in meeting others.

Of course you'll want him to pull on the leash—this is how he tells you where he wants to go and shows you that he's a spirited canine. Just run to keep up with him and get cortisone shots in your elbow if necessary.

Coming When Called:
Breaking a Bad Habit

Most puppies are hard-wired to come when called, but fortunately they tend to outgrow this nasty habit at about four months old. If for some reason your dog still comes when called when he's past the young puppy stage, implement the steps below to nip this behavior in the bud.

1. **Call your dog when he doesn't want to come.** Wait until your dog is completely engrossed in something, like playing with another dog at the dog park or barking at the mailman. After you're sure that there's no chance he'll actually choose you over the object of his attention, say, "Come!" in a demanding, angry voice. If he ignores you, good: you've just taught him that "Come!" means "You don't have to come."

Doggy High-Tech

If you're a dog owner who loves to buy the latest gadgets, there's plenty out there for your IBD.

- **For the escape artist:** Let your dog escape with impunity: there's finally IBD GPS. The Global Pet Finder collar device beams its coordinates for online mapping.

- **For the neurotic:** With the PetsCell collar phone, you can talk to your pet any time. It auto-answers, so paw size doesn't matter!

- **For the barker:** Understand what your dog is trying to say while the neighbors are complaining. A gadget called Bowlingual translates dog sounds into emotions or needs, while a Korean telephone company, SK Telecom, offers a translation service that not only goes dog-to-human but also human-to-dog!

- **For the sex-crazed:** An international online dating site for dogs, www.doggie-dating.co.uk, advertises mating readiness, while www.dog ster.com is MySpace for canines.

- **For the exhibitionist:** Why put all that energy into cultivating your IBD if you can't watch the fun? Pet-cam services allow you to turn your webcam into a 24-hour online viewing device. Or you could buy the iSeePet, a feeder with a webcam built right in.

2. **If, by accident, he does come, ignore him completely.** Don't pet him, don't praise him, and don't make eye contact with him no matter how much he wants your attention. Refrain from any interaction with him until he wanders off. Then wait five minutes and call him again.

3. **Call your dog when you have to do something unpleasant.** Make sure you call your dog to come immediately before you do something he dislikes, such as taking him to the vet or clipping his toenails. Hopefully he'll begin to associate the word "come" with things he'd like to avoid and soon run to hide in response.

4. **Teach your dog that the command "Come" precedes a game of catch-me.** If you call your dog and he doesn't come, run after him. Chasing games are very fun for dogs, particularly when they are

unleashed in public around heavy traffic. Screaming "Come!" louder and louder as he slips from your grasp increases the excitement and effectiveness of the game.

Ball of Destruction

As mentioned in the section above outlining the evils of crates, if you don't encourage destruction in your IBD, not only will he fail to achieve his full dogness, you will not experience the benefit of freedom of detachment from material possessions. An adventuresome dog is a happy dog. Dogs who are encouraged to creatively explore their environments are healthier and more contented, and at times this resourcefulness will include destructive behavior.

The best way to encourage creative canine play is to treat all household objects as your dog's possessions. There should be no distinguishing factor between what's his and what isn't. Remember, it's *all* his. Your dog should be encouraged to believe that everything in the house is fair game. Cashmere sweater? Dog bed. Newspaper? Tug-of-war toy.

Sometimes dogs who have lived for a long time under "traditional" rules have a hard time unlearning the conditioning they received as puppies. They've been brainwashed into believing that dogs are only allowed to handle things that stay on the ground, while everything else in the house belongs to humans. You can undo this by putting his toys on tables and chairs, within his reach but not on the floor, and by giving him your old possessions to play with. He won't know the difference between old socks and new socks, so he'll quickly graduate to chewing up the good ones.

The Well-Rounded IBD

Now that you've got basic skills instilled, you're well on your way to having a top-notch IBD. Even though you're probably already unbearably proud (of yourself as well as your precious pup), there's more. What's next? Advanced IBD behavior!

CHAPTER 8
ADVANCED I.B.D. SKILLS: CROTCH-SNIFFING AND BEYOND

AS WE EXPLORE EVEN MORE progressive concepts to cultivate in the IBD, it's important not to forget the basic tenets of canine behavior modification as outlined in chapter 6: reward heavily and often for those ill behaviors that you'd like your dog to repeat. Sometimes, once the fundamental skills are in place, owners ease off on reinforcement. While it's true that at this point you've already got a competent IBD, if you want to go to the next level, don't allow yourself any slack. With advanced behaviors, life with the IBD just gets more interesting, fun, and all-consuming, so why deny yourself this level of development? In this chapter, we're going to show you:

- How to encourage your dog to urinate on your guests.

- Why begging really *is* cute after all.

- How to encourage your dog to protect your car.

- A few extremely advanced behaviors for the truly adventurous IBD and her owner.

Crotch-Sniffing, Humping, and Marking Strangers

You've probably noticed that dogs sniff one another's private parts. While this may seem invasive to humans, for dogs, that's where all the good stuff is—glands and hormones that communicate such information as gender, whether the dog has been spayed or neutered or is pregnant, if the dog is healthy, even what the dog eats. Of course, a dog's nose is many times stronger than a humans, so it's her primary mode of taking in the world. Why wouldn't dogs want to get to know humans in this way? Crotch-sniffing is the canine equivalent of shaking hands and asking, "Have we met?" When your dog greets a stranger, allow her to explore her sense of smell. Don't accidentally correct her; instead, affectionately repeat the dog's name, smile with embarrassment, and make excuses.

Humping is another dramatic behavior that can best be encouraged by actively following the dominance-permission program detailed in chapter 5 as well as by avoiding any accidental humping aversives. If your dog is a humper, he will likely be humping toy animals, pillows, and other dogs

IBD Hall of Fame: Nuzzle Harassment

In 1997, a class-action lawsuit was filed against a Connecticut judge, alleging that he sexually harassed women and violated their constitutional rights by allowing his golden retriever, Kodak, to "aggressively nuzzle" and "project his snout upward" under their skirts in the courtroom. Fortunately for IBDs everywhere, the district judge who heard the case ruled that the women were "barking up the wrong tree."

already. It's not a big leap for him to include people in this humping behavior. Protest enough to assuage your friends, but not enough to deter your dog.

Marking strangers (peeing on them) is one of the hardest behaviors to encourage in IBDs, only because a successful dog will sadly be rewarded with a swift kick, a substantial enough aversive to forever quell the behavior. Unneutered males excel most at this behavior, which you can foster by allowing your dog to urinate on walks whenever and wherever he pleases. An intact male who is allowed and encouraged to mark his territory will often mistake a human leg for a post or tree. If you're lucky enough to achieve this behavior with your IBD, don't try to stop him in the middle of his business. Instead, focus on helping the person to clean up afterward.

Begging for Food

Current trends discourage begging. This recent prejudice in no way detracts from what people have thought for millennia: it's cute, a great way to bond with your dog, and, of course, the very motivation that brought dogs and humans together in the first place (see chapter 4, "What Do They Really Want? Understanding Your IBD's Drives").

Fortunately, begging is one of the easiest behaviors to instill. Don't stop at the cute begging, however, particularly the kind where a little dog sits up and poses on her hind legs. Instead, go to the next level: the demanding beggar.

The demanding beggar is the one whose desires are satisfied almost all the time, not the dog who has to sing for her supper. The demanding beggar is a properly cultivated IBD who believes she is dominant. Your food is her food. If your dog even looks at you while you have food in your hand, share it. By feeding your dog bits and pieces of anything you're eating, or by dropping food near the table at dinner, you'll soon have a dog that will not only beg for anything, she'll also push the point.

Counter-Surfing and Foraging

A dog who forages for her food is far more stimulated than one who simply finds it every morning in the food dish. To alleviate boredom and improve overall mental health, zookeepers and biologists provide wild animals in captivity with "food puzzles" the animals must solve to obtain their food. This stimulation and satisfaction of the foraging impulse is so important that the USDA has mandated the use of "foraging or task-oriented feeding methods" in its "Laws, Regulations, and Policies for Environmental Enhancement for Nonhuman Primates." Why deprive our canine friends of the same opportunities?

Teach your dog that rewards come to those who look. Dogs can often unearth long-forgotten morsels of food that we have carelessly left behind in trash cans, compost buckets, and fast-food containers on the coffee table. Leave full garbage bags on the floor because you're too lazy to take them out to the curb just yet. Most likely, by the time you're ready, your dog will already have taken advantage of the foraging opportunity!

The easiest place to practice foraging, however, is the kitchen counter. Once your IBD finds that this locale is a predictable and lucrative source of food, you will quickly have a dog who freely grazes off your Corian.

The Smart IBD

Scientists in Germany have proved that dogs know whether we're watching them and are very attuned to our eyes. In the study, if dogs were being watched, they took indirect, deliberately secretive approaches to stealing forbidden food. When researchers appeared to be engrossed in a computer game or had their eyes shut, however, dogs went directly to forbidden food and stole twice as much.

If you have a small dog, leave a chair in a location where she might use it as a jumping point, thus encouraging better exploration of her environment. Over time, be sure that this behavior is reinforced by occasionally leaving such aromatic foods as sliced roast beef near the edge of the counter.

Encourage your dog to help you clean up by licking the food off dishes that have been loaded into the dishwasher. Not only is this exciting and fun for your dog, it also saves wear and tear on your dishwasher. Simply load the dishes up and leave the door to the dishwasher down. This behavior never fails to impress guests at a dinner party!

Riding in the Car with Your IBD

Riding in the car with an IBD can become one of the most exciting parts of your day.

Bolstered by the false sense of confidence an elevated auto provides, dogs can be encouraged to become absolute tyrants in the car. Barking, howling, and aggressive behavior toward approaching humans or dogs is not uncommon, particularly if you've previously instilled in your dog a strong repertoire of defensive and neurotic behaviors.

Dogs should never be confined or tied up while in the car; this would limit their freedom and pleasure. Instead, you learn how to drive in ways that accommodate your dog's wanderings, even if they include stepping on your lap and obscuring your line of vision.

Although some people will tell you that dogs shouldn't ride with their heads sticking out of the car windows, your dog's palpable pleasure at doing so will tell you that denying such a fulfilling activity would be nothing short of cruel. In fact, dogs should be encouraged to explore beyond the window—which of course should be fully open.

Encourage your IBD to guard the car aggressively by leaving her alone in the car while you go shopping with the windows cracked open. If you've spent the time to anti-socialize your dog, she will most likely be leery of passersby. To develop this quality, start off by parking away from areas with lots of foot traffic so she doesn't become conditioned to people walking by the car. Then, when you later switch to more crowded areas, she will no doubt respond by vigorously protecting her mobile home.

Escaping from the House

Dogs love to explore the outside world. In fact, before we shifted into this litigious,

Rosco, an American bulldog living in Virginia Beach, gets the Houdini prize. During a 2006 stay in an animal-control facility, he chewed open the latch to his kennel and climbed over a 7-foot concrete wall topped with barbed wire. When he was caught the next day swimming in a lake some four miles away, Rosco turned himself in without incident.

keep-to-yourself world we live in today, not to mention the proliferation of dangerous-to-dogs cars, dogs roamed freely in their neighborhoods. They hung out on the front porch and wandered wherever they chose. That was a golden age for dogs, and we can have it again—why, after all, should your IBD be held hostage to your schedule?

Dogs will naturally wander from home, particularly if there's a good reason. Small dogs find it thrilling to dart out the front door when a delivery or guest arrives. If you go chase her, loudly calling her name, it's even more exciting to evade capture. Make sure that you encourage this game of catch-me-if-you-can by accidentally leaving the front door open on occasion.

Your IBD will also enjoy dismantling or circumventing the barriers between her and the outside world. Accepted encouragement techniques include:

- **Climbing fences.** Make your fence low enough for your dog to jump over. Wire or chain link is easier for a dog to negotiate than wood or cinder block. If you must install wood, make sure that there are cross-bars applied to at convenient intervals to facilitate traction.

- **Digging under fences and gates.** A nicely aerated section of fresh topsoil will encourage dogs to dig. Avoid wire mesh, gravel, concrete, and rocks under your fences as they can deter your dog from further excavation.

- **Unlatching gates.** A simple gate latch is easy for many dogs to open, provided that they are able to reach it. Make sure that you move the latch to waist height if you have a smaller dog, thus encouraging active jumping. Under no circumstances should you clip the gate with a lock or snap.

Identifying Opportunities for Even More Ill Behavior

After learning all the techniques outlined in this book, you may feel that your dog could not get any worse. We're happy to tell you that you're wrong! We've merely scratched the surface of the universe of possible poor behaviors. With your understanding of the fundamentals, you'll have no trouble introducing the following behaviors to your IBD:

- Climbing fences (chain link work best for novice dogs).

- Ferociously guarding children from their parents.

- Dismantling motors in Jacuzzi tubs (the outer shell must first be destroyed in order to access the motor).

- Eating holes in drywall.

- Chewing up door handles.

- Herding guests into one room and holding them hostage.

- Obsessively fixating on dust particles.

- Screaming (half whine, half howl).

- Anorexia.

- Extreme smoke-detector phobias.

- Uprooting the wall-to-wall carpet.

- Murdering livestock.

- Consuming other household pets.

These are all actual, verified problems seen in exceptional IBDs! But if these don't spur your imagination and you've plateaued in your IBD development, consider sending your dog away to a friend or relative for a few days. A week with a permissive uncle can do wonders for poor behavior! As our

IBDs' constant companions, we unwittingly develop unconscious repetitive habits as we interact with our dogs; a small absence can give your dog the time and space she needs to come up with ever more imaginative poor behaviors.

Creativity Above All

As you probably gleaned from this last section, ingenuity is a tremendously important factor in maintaining the momentum of your IBD's progress. At this point, however, you've given your dog the tools and self-reliance she needs to choose her own IBD path, and soon she'll make the worst decisions for herself. But it's not over yet—in the next chapter, you're going to learn about the holy grails of ill behavior: neurosis and aggression.

THUS FAR WE'VE LED YOU THROUGH fairly standard IBD behaviors. Now, in our last instructional section, we're going to share with you secrets of the *ne plus ultra* of the IBD: a dog who is either categorically crazy or aggressively dangerous. Who would want such dogs? Recall the dog-owning types of chapter 2. Generally owners with their own neurotic tendencies—especially those motivated to own dogs as replacement humans or therapists—cultivate dogs with neuroses. And, as you might guess, owners who are compensating for their own inadequacies prize the violent, aggressive IBD. We do have to warn you that violent IBDs can cause problems. As famed Supreme Court justice Oliver Wendell Holmes Jr., stated, "The right to swing my fist ends where the other man's nose begins." As all of us know, however, there will always be individuals compensating for their own inadequacies by fostering aggression in their IBDs, and if they choose to do so, they might as well do it right. In this chapter, we'll show you:

- How to leave the house in a way that maximizes separation anxiety.

- How your IBD can learn new neuroses at doggy daycare.

- Why you should immediately caress your dog if he's barking, growling, or snarling.

- Why you should leave your IBD in the front yard.

Separation Anxiety: The Spoils of Codependence

Separation anxiety is the hottest new disorder among canines, and luckily, it's one of the easiest to encourage. Dogs are becoming more and more neurotic, in no small part due to our lifestyles. No longer can dogs just loll about, entertaining themselves in the backyard. Instead, the modern dog spends the majority of his time in the house, waiting for you to return without any stimulation or access to exercise while you are gone. This kind of environment is ripe for developing a good case of separation anxiety.

A dog that cannot function without you is prone to all kinds of poor behaviors, including chewing things that smell like you, gnawing on the furniture, urinating inside the house, barking until the neighbors complain, clawing doors and jambs, boring holes in the

Just Say No

Dogs are right behind people when it comes to the prevalence of psychotropic drugs—antidepressants, antianxiety medications, and so forth. Since the passing of a 1994 act legalizing the treatment of pets with human drugs not approved for animals ("off-label use"), this anti-IBD medical trend is on the rise.

Drug	Human Ailments Treated	Canine Ailments Treated
Prozac	Depression, OCD, bulimia, panic disorder	Separation anxiety
Clomicalm	Depression, OCD	Noise phobia, separation anxiety
Valium	Anxiety disorders	Separation anxiety, phobias
Lithium carbonate	Bipolar disorder	Aggression

drywall, climbing fences, and even launching himself through the windows and doors.

If your dog exhibits none of these reactions and seems placid around your departures and returns, here are a few easy ways to encourage separation anxiety:

- **Make comings and goings extremely emotional.** Highly charged outpourings are the key to developing a strong anxious response in your absence. When you leave, swoon over your dog, petting and doting on him, telling him you'll be back soon. When you return, make the reunion extremely exciting by ferociously petting your dog and speaking to him in a high-pitched, excited voice, allowing him to jump on you and lick you all over. These episodes create a sharp contrast between your presence and your absence, a critical dynamic to developing the correct pattern of anxiety.

- **Ritualize your exits.** Develop a routine of collecting your keys and putting on your coat to cue your dog that you're about to leave so he can work up to the maximum anxiety level. Your dog must know you're gone in order to fall to pieces, so sneaking out will not help instill separation anxiety.

- **Leave your dog with nothing to do.** If you provide your IBD with chew toys, bones, or anything else with which he can distract himself, he may not remember to become anxious.

- **Encourage intense bonding with your dog.** Make sure your dog plays *the* central role in your life. Let him sleep in bed with you, cuddle often, and revolve your day around him and his needs. Lavish him with affection, treats, and constant attention. The goal is to have him believe that without you present, his world will fall apart. This does not, however, work with boyfriends.

The Obsessive-Compulsive IBD

Dogs that exhibit what some owners might call "obsessive-compulsive disorder" are truly fascinating to watch. Unfortunately, these traits are very difficult to cultivate in dogs that don't have a genetic predisposition for OCD; indeed, OCD is thought to result from inbreeding, especially in such breeds as German shepherds, rottweilers, dalmatians, and bulldogs. Canine OCD manifests itself as fixations, repetitive behaviors that the dog cannot seem to stop (called stereotypies), and self-mutilation. For example, some dogs will hunt for lost objects to the exclusion of all other activities, even eating. Others incessantly pace, lick themselves until they create sores, or chase their tails.

OCD behavior is frequently found in dogs with high hunt and prey drives, lots of energy, and very little else to do. These OCD tendencies are, ironically, an excellent quality to have in dogs used for search-and-rescue or drug detection because they are single-minded about the task at hand. Indeed, German shepherds, prime OCD candidates, are most often used for police work. If you're lucky enough to have one of these dogs, bore them to tears and then hide their ball.

The Glory of Whining

Whining is a one of the best neurotic behaviors to encourage in the IBD because once the behavior has been instilled, it's almost impossible to stop. Promote whining by crating your dog. When he begins to vocalize, immediately reward him by opening the crate door.

Many dogs will whimper quietly, but your goal is a plaintive wail. To encourage more

IBD Hall of Fame: Pro-NRA Canines

Poor canine behavior isn't limited to the damage that can be wrought with teeth and paws. Like their owners, a select few champion IBDs manage to make themselves heard with guns.

Many dog-shoots-human incidents occur while hunting. In Minnesota, for example, an English setter named Sonny stepped on the trigger of a loaded gun and shot his owner in the ankle as the victim posed with fellow hunters for a photo. A German hunter was fatally shot in his vehicle when his dog jumped into the car and landed on a gun that the owner had placed on the seat. In Bulgaria, an owner became enraged at his dog, who would not release a retrieved dead bird, and began beating the dog with a rifle. Fortunately, the dog's paw caught the trigger and gave the man his due.

Indeed, one of the most dramatic dog-shoots-man stories is one of self-defense. In 2004, a Florida man determined to shoot seven puppies because he couldn't find them a home. After three had been killed, a fourth wriggled his way to the trigger of the gun and shot the man in the wrist. The man was charged with animal cruelty and the puppies were adopted, hopefully by owners who recognized their IBD potential.

varied and expressive whining, utilize the principle of the jackpot theory (see chapter 6, "Rewards and Deterrents: Ill-Behavior Modification"). When your dog gives a particularly mournful cry, reward. Your dog will soon learn that the more heart-wrenching pleas get him out of the crate sooner.

To generalize this behavior to the outside world, teach your IBD that whining will get him what he wants. If he whines at the door, drop everything and take him for a walk. If he whines at the vet, remove him from the exam room and go home. If he whines at the refrigerator, give him a steak.

Effective Reinforcement for Barking and Growling

Barking is a universal dog behavior that every IBD should know. Most dogs naturally bark at strange noises at night or at the sound of the doorbell ringing. If you catch your dog barking, praise him well and encourage it with a lively "Yes, Fido!" Even calling his name out and telling him to be quiet will accomplish your goals.

If you don't have a naturally gifted barker, you can often create one by allowing your dog to hang out with a barker, as barking lends itself well to mimicking. One of the best places to find good barkers is at doggy daycare. These facilities usually have many different kinds of dogs, so there's bound to be a good barker among them. Visit the daycares in your area ahead of time to ascertain which is the loudest. Within a few days, your dog will learn to bark confidently, and with any luck he'll transfer that behavior to his home environment.

Bona Fide Neuroses

Your IBD has at his disposal a wide variety of specific anxieties and neuroses. While many have some genetic origin, these conditions can all be encouraged by providing your dog with as few social opportunities and as little exercise as possible.

Diagnosis	Description
Acral lick dermatitis	Obsessively licking, usually on paws or legs, that results in skin lesions.
Astraphobia	Fear of thunderstorms.
Coprophagia	Ingesting feces.
Displaced sex drive	Humping invisible mates.
Firework phobia	Fear of fireworks.
Pica	Ingesting nonfood items such as rocks, drywall, and socks.
Spinning (tail-chasing)	Compulsive spinning in circles, often for hours on end.
Submissive urination	Urination when faced with uncomfortable social contact.

Rewarding Displays of Aggression

When dogs bark and growl, they're trying to communicate, which should always be actively encouraged. Dogs will naturally display aggression when faced with threats, and barking followed by growling are often precursors to snapping, biting, or fighting. In order to encourage this behavior, you must present your dog with threats then teach him that by acting aggressively, the threats are neutralized. Here are some easy exercises to promote aggressive behavior:

1. **Present your dog with a "threat" such as a strange visitor.** Hopefully, your previous anti-socialization has resulted in your dog perceiving anyone outside your home as a potential threat. Dogs with a high defensive drive will also be quick to judge strangers as threats.

2. **Pet your dog.** When your dog reacts aggressively by barking, growling, or snarling, kneel down, pet him calmly, and say, "Easy, easy." This will communicate to your dog that aggression is the correct response.

3. **Remove the threat.** Either wait until the "threat" moves away or drag your barking dog off. This teaches the dog that displays of aggression work. Threats go away.

Cultivating Overprotectiveness

Like humans, dogs display aggression around items they perceive as valuable; as this is a natural defensive tendency, it will probably arise of its own volition if you cultivate other aggressive, territorial behaviors. Not only will your overprotective IBD guard things he *should* guard (like your house), he'll extend this behavior to guard other things. A dog who guards what most people would deem inappropriate is not only ill-behaved, he's neurotic—a grand slam! Examples of overprotected objects include children, other household pets, laundry, Christmas gifts, and even the toilet.

Territorial Aggression: Maximum K-9 Defense at Home

Most dogs will naturally exhibit some degree of territorial aggression if they've lived long enough in one spot to establish a territory. Even dogs who have particularly small territories (for example, dogs who are chained up) are vigilant about protecting their small patch of the universe. Here's how to encourage vicious displays of aggression against potential intruders:

Doggy Dictionary: Bark Mitzvah

In the Jewish tradition, a bark mitzvah welcomes your IBD into adulthood with a gala thirteenth-birthday celebration.

- **Leave your dog in the front yard.** Dogs in front yards are much more likely to become aggressive than dogs in backyards simply because there is more traffic for your dog to defend against.

- **Promote visual contact.** Allow visual contact with potential intruders, but keep your dog behind the fence. A transparent fence is much better than a solid one because it allows for visual stimulation.

- **Install a large bay window.** If you don't have a front yard, a bay window looking out onto traffic is a necessity. This will allow your dog to run back and forth along the window, defending your house from passersby and potentially dangerous individuals. If you have a small dog, a sofa placed under the window will allow him to jump up and survey the territory from a normal height, thus bolstering his confidence.

- **Get a second dog.** There is nothing better to encourage aggressive displays than a second dog. Even relatively meek dogs will feed off the self-assurance of another dog and join in when it comes time to protect their territory.

Who Needs Prozac?

It's hard to believe veterinarians are prescribing ever-increasing quantities of canine antidepressants and antianxiety medications—who would want to extinguish the kinds of fascinating behaviors you've just learned about? Apparently, quite a few people, dog lovers and haters alike, *do* want to limit your IBD rights. And that's what we'll address in the final chapter, because no doubt after experiencing this process you'll want to become an IBD advocate.

CHAPTER 10
CONCLUSION:
I.B.D. LOVERS UNITE!

CONGRATULATIONS, IBD LOVER—
you've done it! After lots of hard but enjoy-
able work, you've cultivated your very own
IBD. Once you've lived with an IBD for a
while, you'll probably start to notice that not
everybody appreciates your approach to dog
behavior. In fact, there are looming naysay-
ers who seek to curtail your IBD rights.
After appreciating the joys of the IBD, you'll
want to spread the word and garner support
for this complex companion animal.

There are many reasons to agitate for the
IBD cause. Enemies of the IBD include
landlords, neighbors, passersby, and even
other dog owners in such venues as dog

parks. Your neighbors can get an injunction against your barking IBD or take you to small-claims court and force you to pay damages for their lost sleep or quality of life. There's even a type of lawyer known as a dog-bite attorney! From leash laws to pooper-scooper rules to outlawed breeds to mandatory sterilization, your rights as a dog owner are under constant attack.

United IBD lovers stand, divided they fall, so you'll want to go out into the world and find others who share your special beliefs. Until the movement gathers strength, the best way to find like-minded souls is to patronize places where dogs gather, especially dog parks. At these parks, take the opportunity to observe how others behave with their dogs (since you won't be watching yours, you'll be free to look around). You'll be able to identify other dog owners who don't keep an eye on their dogs, encourage aggression, or repeat ineffectual commands. Approach those people and let them know about your commitment to the IBD. Tell them how well your household runs now that your IBD is the center of the universe. Before you know it, you'll have a support group that could one day become a political action committee!

As an IBD owner and advocate, there's only one more thing to do. Think back to the "Multiple-Dog Households" section of chapter 3. Now that you've accomplished one IBD, don't you think it's time for another?

Canine Quip

"Many have forgotten this truth, but you must not forget it. You become responsible forever for what you have tamed."

—Antoine de Saint-Exupery